A MOSAIC OF FAITH

A Mosaic of Faith

11 Lessons Jesus Taught His Disciples

W.L. Seaver

WingSpread Publishers

Camp Hill, Pennsylvania

WingSpread Publishers
Camp Hill, Pennsylvania
www.wingspreadpublishers.com

A division of Zur Ltd.

A Mosaic of Faith: 11 Lessons Jesus Taught His Disciples
ISBN: 978-1-60066-296-6
LOC Control Number: 2012932971
© 2009, 2012 by W.L. Seaver

16 15 14 13 12   5 4 3 2 1

Cover design by Pencil Tip Design

Contents

Preface

This book is not an autobiographical exposition about my faith or anyone else's faith in God. It is an attempt to define the faith in God as illustrated, taught and extolled in the Gospels. Having been involved in some sort of ministry for almost forty years, such as a university ministry, college athletic ministry, discipleship ministry among men in the workplace, various church ministries at all ages, small group ministries, full-time pastor and as a professor who is excited about his faith on campus, my soul has been troubled about the lack of faith, the stagnant faith or the weak faith that I have witnessed in others and in myself.

As a result, I started my own personal study of faith in the Gospels, and the interchanges about faith between Jesus and His disciples and between Jesus and others with the disciples looking on. Many have encouraged me to put the series to print to pass onto others who may need to reassess their faith in God or who may not really have faith in God but have gone through the motions of religion without a personal relationship with Jesus Christ as their Savior. Others who might benefit are those who need encouragement in their faith or who really desire their faith in a great God to grow even more in His way and in His time.

As a result of this need to evaluate or reassess our faith in God, examples of faith from my life or the lives of others are sparsely interwoven into this book. There are two reasons for this. The first reason is based on parts of Exodus and Numbers with the need for water. The first time, God provided water for the sons of Israel by commanding Moses to strike the rock, after which the waters came forth abundantly (Exodus 17). And the second time in Numbers 20, God told Moses to speak to the rock, but in Moses' impatience he struck the rock again. God provided water because the need of the people and animals was more important than dealing with Moses right then. The third time the Israelites were to sing and dig for water (Numbers 21).

On three different occasions, God saw fit to provide for the need of water in three different ways so that the trust of those people would be in Him and not the method. I am very concerned that people might construe my examples and how God led and acted for others or me by thinking that is what He will do for them.

The second reason for few examples is to put my personality in the background and allow the face of Christ to shine brightly. The essence of each chapter is to expound the biblical text and the flow of events coming up to the teachable moment. At the end of each chapter (except chapters 1 and 14) are sections entitled "Life Response to Biblical Truth" and "Questions for Reflection." These sections delineate applications or insights about the truths that need to be personally considered or applied.

This is not one of those books to be read at one or two sittings. As with studying the Gospels, one needs to move thoughtfully and prayerfully through each chapter, slowly, under the power of the Holy Spirit, asking God to help the reader hear His voice. If one were studying a chapter per week, one might choose one application to meditate on each day. It is the author's desire that this book be read not once but many times. Maybe on each reading God will prick your heart, as He does mine, to focus on a specific application that is pertinent at the moment.

Finally, this book was not designed to replace anyone's time in studying the Word of God. Rather, my intent is to help readers evaluate where their faith is, but most importantly, where our eyes of faith need to be focused. This book is not a complete treatise on faith; instead, it looks at faith as specifically mentioned in the Gospels. This study of faith has caused me to stand in amazement of my Savior and the wonder of His ways and timing. In other words, our focus on God and obedience to His Word should become more intense but relaxed. We must remember to "cease striving and know that I am God" (Psalm 46:10).

Chapter 1

Faith beyond the Gospels and Acts

A.W. Tozer said,

> Real faith is not the stuff dreams are made of; rather it is tough, practical and altogether realistic. Faith sees the invisible but it does not see the nonexistent. Faith engages God, the one great Reality, who gave and gives existence to all things. God's promises conform to reality, and whoever trusts them enters a world not of fiction but of fact.[1]

This real faith is not found in people, programs, organization, traditions, marketing or emotionalism. It is found in God and His Word. Of course, if someone doesn't know Jesus Christ as his Savior and Lord, he cannot walk by faith in anything that he does. Many believers, however, fail to walk by faith because they trust in what works (i.e., a tendency to do things in a practical manner and not in what God says). For instance, suppose you met someone at an athletic club who is only in town for a few days because his parents were moving. After the workout, you talked and had a good conversation; but later that afternoon the Holy Spirit burdened your soul that you should have shared the gospel with the individual. Would you spend several hours trying to find this individual and then share the good news with him? This may not be practical, but obedience here would be an act of faith.

Or suppose a young family with two young children needs a larger car. They live in a small, rural town about an hour from a larger town. They need to buy a larger car to handle their family transportation needs, but they need to sell their sporty car quickly to be faithful with God's money. They expected their sporty car to sell quickly since it was in excellent condition; but as they prayed about selling the sporty car, God convicted them that they were trusting in their car and not in Him. As a result of this conviction and more praying, God impressed on them another way to sell the car that would require more faith in Him. They could run an ad in the large town newspaper for buyers to come see the car only on Saturday in that town. This may not be practical, but if they were acting on faith, wouldn't they drive the car that is to be sold and either borrow or rent another car so that they have transportation back home? Does not real faith see the invisible God as able to do exceedingly beyond what we ask or think (Ephesians 3:20)? Suppose the buyer of the car wants the owner to say that the purchase price is only $3,000 instead of $10,000 so that he can save money on taxes. Does the owner compromise and gain the sale, or does he hold the line about being honest and trust God to make the sale anyway? This entire experience was a journey in the realm of faith!

In each of these cases, tough choices need to be made to bring glory to God and to be obedient to His Word. These quick illustrations reveal that the essence of walking by faith should encompass all phases of life, a lesson that the disciples had to learn and that we need to continually be reminded of. It is this essence of faith that is revealed in the Gospels. The rest of the New Testament and the Old Testament also have much to say about faith in God and His Word. The intent of the author is to make it clear to the reader that a study on our faith in God and how God grows our faith would take many books and might be wearying to the soul to read. A list of key verses in the New Testament on faith or on the believer being faithful is provided in the appendix at the end of the book. This list may not be exhaustive, but it captures the essence of faith mentioned outside the Gospels and the book of Acts and its importance to our Father in heaven.

The list is provided for the reader's self-study and edification.

A close study of the list would indicate that the book of Romans has the most to say about faith, followed by Hebrews (which is not surprising because of Hebrews chapter 11, the "Hall of Fame" chapter on faith). On the other hand, relative to the number of chapters in an epistle, Galatians and 1 Timothy have the greater incidence of faith citations. The easiest way to study the essence of faith would be to study these two epistles of Paul. The coverage of living by faith, however, is best initiated by examining the book of Habakkuk.

Habakkuk and Faith

The key verse in Habakkuk about faith is chapter 2, verse 4: "The righteous will live by his faith." The context of this verse arises out of Habakkuk's struggle with the unfathomable ways of God. The prophet Habakkuk was heavily burdened by the wickedness of Judah. The law was being ignored, justice was never upheld, the wicked hemmed in the righteous, and there was a general perversion of justice (Habakkuk 2:1–4).

Habakkuk questioned God about how long this perversion would go on and why He did not do something about it. God in turn answered that He would send the Chaldeans or the Babylonians to chastise Judah. However, this divine response triggered more questions about why God would use the wicked (Babylonians) to correct the seemingly more righteous (Judah). There is no immediate answer from God, and this is one of the first things we learn about faith: In the realm of living by faith, it takes faith to wait on God to answer prayers or questions. It takes faith to wait on Him to give instructions as to what to do and when to do it and sometimes to learn that the most difficult thing to do is to do nothing. God's eventual answer to Habakkuk then and to us now is: "Behold, as for the proud one, his soul is not right within him; but the righteous will live by his faith" (Habakkuk 2:4).

Simply stated, there are two kinds of people: the proud and the righteous. The proud is obviously not trusting in God but in him or herself. In contrast, the righteous one is trusting in God and Scripture and not in self. A believer is walking by faith and faith alone in God, but the soul of the proud is not right within him. This assessment of the soul not being right within the individual is an assessment that our Father in heaven can easily make within His omniscience.

It is interesting that this key passage in Habakkuk on living by faith does not provide a list of faith activities or responsibilities or attitudes that one could just check off to enable one to say that "I have kept all these things from my youth up" (Mark 10:17–22), as the rich young ruler responded to Jesus. Such a list would encourage living by the power of the flesh and not by faith in the power of the Holy Spirit. The essence of living by faith is trust in God's Word and His person. The soul of such a one who lives this way would be right before God.

But the soul of the proud is not right with God. Telltale signs of a self-sufficient individual who does not or will not trust God include restlessness as well as greed or insatiable appetite for things like control, fame, entertainment or power. The self-sufficient person is never satisfied with what he has, where he has come from or what he looks like. These people are always trying to conquer, control or manipulate others for self-gain or self-exaltation.

The one who walks by faith has a rest in God and seeks God and His kingdom, knowing that all needs will be provided by the Father in heaven. Unlike the proud, the righteous one is content in his circumstances and does not have to scheme or control others to accomplish his ends since the ultimate end is to know and bring glory to God.

This contrast of the proud and the righteous in Habakkuk seems to be a stark comparison of non-believers (Babylonians) with righteous believers. There are many believers today, however, who have begun the life of faith properly by placing their faith in Jesus Christ as the only provision for their sin; but as noted by the Apostle Paul, they have begun by the Spirit but are now trying to perfect themselves by the flesh (Galatians 2:3). Outwardly, they may look like the proud one described in Habakkuk 2:4–5.

It is too easy for the believer today to trust in education, intelligence, human strength, lineage, the ability to create fear in others, the manipulations of others, organization abilities, money—or anything other than God Himself. Jesus saw these same tendencies in the disciples He chose to be with Him. As we look at the divine record in the Gospels, we will see Jesus' methods and timing of events to mold and mature these disciples to be men of faith.

Critical Passages on Faith in the Gospels

Eleven events recorded in the Gospels directly deal with faith, and the disciples are present at each of these events. Generally, sermons and teaching from these passages have been done in an isolated way, but there is much more to be gained pedagogically by examining not only the individual events pertaining to faith but also the interrelationship between these events over time. Each chapter to follow examines one of these eleven events and looks at the relationship between that event and preceding events. Chapters 13 and 14 explore the interrelationships between all eleven events on faith. For the purpose of self-study, readers are encouraged to meditate on and study the passages of Scripture given at the beginning of each chapter *prior* to reading the chapter.

A quick perusal of these eleven unique events reveals that nine of them are recorded in the Gospel of Matthew, seven in Mark and seven in Luke. Not one of the events is recorded in the Gospel of John, but the purpose of John's Gospel was that "you may believe that Jesus is the Christ, the Son of God; and that believing you may have life in His name" (John 20:31). The remaining chapters of this book about growing in faith may not be very productive if the reader is without a personal faith in Jesus Christ as Savior and Lord (as noted in the Gospel of John). If you do know Jesus Christ as your Redeemer, may the chapters to follow excite your heart and ignite a richer relationship with your God by faith.

Chapter 2

Faith and the Basics of Life

Read Matthew 6:19–34 and Luke 12:22–34

The first place in the Gospels that faith is verbally addressed is in the Sermon on the Mount, which occurred roughly one year into Jesus' ministry with the disciples. Prior to this great event, nine miracles concerning creation, sickness, demons, leprosy, paralysis and deformities had occurred. Faith was exercised in four of the nine cases. In the healing of a nobleman's son (John 4:46–54), for example, this royal official believed Jesus' words and went home. In the miraculous catch of fish (Luke 5:1–11), Peter believed the Lord's words, even though contrary to customary fishing methods and timing. A leper (Mark 1:40–45) and friends of a paralytic also believed in Jesus and His words.

There was no formal teaching on faith or living by faith until the end of the first year of ministry. Why was there such delay? One could speculate *ad infinitum*, but it is very likely that our Lord was focused on proclaiming the good news, the kingdom of God in their midst (Luke 4:17–21, 43–44). It is also highly likely that the Lord was not seeing believers (His disciples) consistently walk by faith even though there were instances in His ministry where faith had been exhibited and even though these saints should have been aware of the words of Habakkuk, "The righteous will live by his faith" (2:4).

It is in this context that our Lord begins to teach and challenge believers. From the 5th chapter of Matthew and the 6th chapter of Luke, one sees that the Lord's words in the Sermon on the Mount were addressed to believers as He gazed on the disciples and began to teach them:

> When Jesus saw the crowds, He went up on the mountain; and after He sat down, His disciples came to Him. He opened His mouth and began to teach them, saying . . . (Matthew 5:1–2)

> Jesus came down with them and stood on a level place; and there was a large crowd of His disciples, and a great throng of people from all Judea and Jerusalem and the coastal region of Tyre and Sidon, who had come to hear Him and to be healed of their diseases; and those who were troubled with unclean spirits were being cured. And all the people were trying to touch Him, for

power was coming from Him and healing them all. And turning His gaze toward His disciples, He began to say . . . (Luke 6:17–20)

These new believers were brought up in a religious system where values, focus, faith and service had all been distorted from what God had intended. They needed to be presented complete in Christ (Colossians 1:28), and it was time to right the ship!

Discouraged Preoccupations

Within the teaching of the Sermon on the Mount the Lord deals with a believer's blessings, witness, attitudes, motives and prayer life, along with priorities on possessions, faith and much more. Jesus' discussion on faith is preceded by His discussion on possessions or treasures on earth as noted below:

> Do not store up for yourselves treasures on earth . . . But store up for yourselves treasures in heaven . . . for where your treasure is, there your heart will be also. The eye is the lamp of the body; so then if your eye is clear, your whole body will be full of light. But if your eye is bad, your whole body will be full of darkness. If then the light that is in you is darkness, how great is the darkness! No one can serve two masters; for either he will hate the one and love the other, or he will be devoted to one and despise the other. You cannot serve God and wealth (mammon). (Matthew 6:19–24)

This part of the Lord's discussion in this section of Matthew chapter 6 assuredly relates to the "men of little faith," who cannot trust God for things like food and clothing. It is not a coincidence that trusting God for the basics in life is critical to pressing on in the life of faith. In the Old Testament books of Exodus and Numbers, the sons of Israel had trouble trusting God for food (manna and quail provided, Exodus 16) and water (Exodus 15 and 17) when leaving Egypt, even with the supernatural presence of God in the cloud during the day and the pillar of fire at night. There was no way of storing manna from day to day, except that on the sixth day the manna lasted an extra day so that the sons of Israel would have a day of rest. It is no different today in that God does not want us storing up for ourselves, but rather managing as wise stewards (Luke 16:1–13) the resources, talents and possessions He has given us.

The preoccupation with possessions or treasures on earth enslaves the heart since there is no way to really protect those treasures without God's assistance. These earthly treasures take time, energy and resources. If God is recognized as the Giver, the Sustainer and the Taker of these treasures (since they are really His anyway), then our faith will not be undermined. On the other hand, to try clinging to these treasures or controlling them (but they actually control us) is an extremely unhealthy preoccupation since it affects our heart. Likewise, this same preoccupation with treasures affects our vision or our focus. The end result is that our souls and minds do not see clearly as God would have us see the events and situations of life. Our vision or focus is preoccupied with how our material things are affected instead of how God's name or glory is impacted. In addition, this preoccupation with stuff and the glory of men saps our strength and diffuses or destroys our service to God.

This unhealthy preoccupation of the heart, this diffused focus of the eye of the soul and this distracted service and misuse of our strength does not happen immediately but in small steps followed by bigger steps. This digression in the spiritual life has steps that are similar to the life of faith but exactly opposite in leading one to trust in oneself more instead of less. This path does not lead to more dependence and more faith in the Savior but less in every way. It is no wonder that our Lord said, "You cannot serve God and wealth (mammon)." May we all rightly assess our preoccupation with treasures on earth, our focus on the divine and the expenditure of our energies so that we can ask for God's help in walking the path of faith!

Divided or Distracted Minds and Hearts

If one is laying up treasures on earth instead of in heaven, this will be evidenced by that person not seeing the events and situations of life as God does and by his or her not having time to serve God due to servitude to things of this life. The telltale evidence of these flaws is revealed in a person's anxiety (distracted or divided minds) as noted by Jesus' words:

> For this reason I say to you, do not be worried about your life, as to what you will eat or what you will drink; nor for your body, as to what you will put on. [1] Is not life more than food, and the body more than clothing? Look at the birds of the air, that they do not sow, nor reap nor gather into barns, and yet your heavenly Father feeds them. Are you not worth much more than they? [2] And who of you by being worried can add a single hour to his life? [3] And why are you worried about clothing? Observe how the lilies of the field grow; they do not toil nor do they spin, yet I say to you that not even Solomon in all his glory clothed himself like one of these. But if God so clothes the grass of the field, which is alive today and tomorrow is thrown into the furnace, will He not much more clothe you? [4] You of little faith! Do not worry then, saying, "What will we eat?" or "What will we drink?" or "What will we wear for clothing?" (Matthew 6:25–31)

Four times in these verses our Lord either exhorted the disciples to not be anxious or queried them on their rationale for anxiety. In Matthew 6:25, we are told to stop worrying. There is a lot in life to worry about, and it is easy to get in the habit of worrying about the basics, such as food, clothing and shelter. Worry and the habit of worrying are contrary to the life of faith, and as such they are clear signs that we are concerned about the things and treasures upon earth. In Matthew 6:31 (also 6:34), the exhortation about worry is to not worry at all about the basics of life. If we worry about the basics of food and clothing, that habit of worrying will become ingrained in our life and translate to other things as well. Such worry is a cancer that destroys a life of faith and undermines the richness of the personal relationship with Christ. We all need to pay strong heed to this command of our Master!

In mathematics, there are optimization methods to find a set of best solutions to a problem when there are certain constraints. This set of solutions is called the feasible set. All of the solutions outside this feasible set are impractical and inappropriate. From the divine perspective, all believers have constraints in life as to talents, resources, etc. The infeasible set of solutions (nonoptimal) to problems and situations leaves God out, while the feasible set of solutions leaves God in the center of it all (optimal). In the feasible set, God has many solutions! The implication of this truth is that ten people may have a similar need or difficult situation, but God could have ten different ways to solve the problem within a feasible set of solutions. Our Lord describes this feasible set with the words "more than" and "much more." There is more to life than food and clothing. We are worth more than the birds. Worrying does not add more to life but subtracts from it. Our Father will do much more for us than we can imagine. Let's look at this supernatural feasible set!

1. **More to life than food and clothing (Matthew 6:25)** Our Lord puts this principle in a question: "Is not life more than food, and the body more than clothing?" The obvious answer to the question is, "Yes, there is more to life than food and clothing." But as believers we worry more about food and clothing, and we miss the "More-to-Life" that is the supernatural feasible set including people, the Word of God, God Himself and things that last for eternity. Absorption with the More-to-Life causes everything else, including food and clothing, to pale in comparison. If we are in the supernatural feasible set, we will be walking by faith. Outside, we are in the fleshy infeasible set, where what we accomplish or value is maintained by human effort and will not last for eternity.

2. **Worth much more (Matthew 6:26)** And when Jesus asks, "Are you not worth much more than they?" again the obvious answer is yes. God provides food and everything else that the birds of the air need. They lack nothing. But we are worth much more than the birds since we have a soul and a spirit and since Jesus died for us. The "worth more" is again the supernatural feasible set. It is only possible for us to see ourselves as worthy if we see ourselves as God does—sinners but redeemed by the Lamb, immature but with potential in Christ if we walk by faith and finite in today's world but with infinite possibil-

ities for eternal value. The Apostle Paul warned us not to think of ourselves more highly than we should, "but to think so as to have sound judgment, as God has allotted to each a measure of faith" (Romans 12:3). Conceited or proud perspectives of our worth are to be avoided, but our worth comes from our Savior and Lord, the value He places on us, and what He has done for us. Our worth is encapsulated by His worth, and that is embraced only by humility and faith.

3. **Add a single cubit to his life's span (Matthew 6:27)** "And who of you by being worried can add a single hour to his life?" is another question from Jesus' lips that is delineating the feasible set of faith. In general, people want to have a long and prosperous life. Yet, worry or anxiety shortens the length and the value of life. Worry puts one in the infeasible set since it does not focus on or understand a sovereign God. The one who does not worry is not distracted or divided in mind or heart but rather rests in the promises of God and the person of God, who is the ultimate "More-to-Life." Again, membership in this supernatural feasible set requires daily walking by faith and cultivating the richness of a personal relationship with Jesus Christ. While worry decreases the quality of both the spiritual life and physical life, living by faith increases them.

4. **Much more from the Father (Matthew 6:30)** If our heavenly Father provides for the lilies and grass of the field, why should we worry about clothing? If God is so concerned about those things that are here today and gone tomorrow, "Will He not much more clothe you? You of little faith!" This supernatural feasible set is the "much more" that the Father can do for us. Sadly, this supernatural feasible set is not experienced by most believers. In Ephesians 3:20, under the inspiration of the Holy Spirit, Paul says, "Now to Him who is able to do exceeding abundantly beyond all that we ask or think . . ." (NASB, 1977).

To enter this supernatural feasible set, one must think God's thoughts and believe what He says in His revealed Word. The mind must be renewed on a daily basis by God's Word and tested by the experiences of life that move us to walk more and more by faith for a closer dependence upon Him. As that occurs, we will not ask with wrong motives. Instead, our prayer life will spring from the supernatural feasible set since we will see things as God sees them. Not only will we see much more done by the Father, but we also will come to know the Father much more intimately through the Son.

Believers in this supernatural feasible set know there is more to life than food and clothing, and they have so ordered their priorities. These believers know their true worth and have a healthy perspective of their value since it is encompassed by the worth of our Lord. They also know that worry or anxiety contribute nothing but negativity and fleshy manipulations that draw us away from the Lord. These same believers also know that there is much more that the Father can and will do for His children if they would just trust Him. Thus, these saints in this supernatural feasible set know there is much more to life. They know that they are worth more, worrying will not add to their life span and their Father in heaven can do exceedingly beyond what they ask or think.

In the Lord's days on earth, the occupants in this supernatural feasible set were generally not the disciples or the people in the know on the spiritual scene. This is evidenced by the Lord's words to these disciples, "You of little faith." Likewise, I doubt that most Christians today occupy the supernatural feasible set since few believe that the proof of your faith is more precious than the perishable:

> That the proof of your faith, being more precious than gold which is perishable, even though tested by fire, may be found to result in praise and glory and honor at the revelation of Jesus Christ. (1 Peter 1:7)

We tend to focus on the gold of this world (which can be in many forms) and what can be done with the gold rather than focusing on the faith of the believer, which is far more precious and valuable than gold. The timing of the Lord's words in the Sermon on the Mount was most poignant in light of the Roman occupation that brought economic, political and social stresses in life. Should we not likewise hunger and strive for the faith that pleases God and not the gold of this age that is perishable?

Divine Model Not the Pagan Model

When Jesus commented about the disciples' little faith in the Sermon on the Mount, it was the first of five times over the next two years that there would be discussion of this topic. The repetition of this discussion reveals that the topic was very important for the kingdom of heaven to advance and that the disciples fell short of understanding the basics of living by a type of faith that permeates all that we are and do. For about one year, our Lord observed the disciples to see that faith and godliness were not being consistently manifested in their lives. As any discipler of men will know, if faith in the Word of God and the person of God is not being manifested on a regular basis over time, corrections are very necessary. The basic truths of Scripture must be understood and applied for a disciple to progress in faith. The Lord had not seen that progression. Thus, the words of our Lord in Matthew's Gospel deliver a new paradigm or a divine model that is contrary to the pagan model accepted by the world:

> Do not worry then, saying, "What will we eat?" or "What will we drink?" or "What will we wear for clothing?" For the Gentiles eagerly seek all these things; for your heavenly Father knows that you need all these things. But seek first His kingdom and His righteousness, and all these things will be added to you. So do not worry about tomorrow; for tomorrow will care for itself. Each day has enough trouble of its own. (Matthew 6:31–34)

The divine model is to be filled with faith and not worry. To be anxious about what we shall eat, drink or wear creates a lifestyle of worry and not faith. The Gentiles or pagans of our day spend great energies in seeking these things as one can easily verify by noting the heavy slant of advertising on food, drinks (soft drinks, beer, etc.) and clothing inclusive of anything related to appearances. The biblical exhortation from the very lips of Jesus, however, is to not be anxious about these basics. Our heavenly Father knows that we need them, and He will provide them. We don't have to be absorbed in and worried about keeping up with the Joneses in appearances or lifestyle. We need to be absorbed in the things of faith, the Word and the person of God. Trust and worry cannot coexist. They are polar opposites, and in fact they are mutually antagonistic since they negate each other. Thus, worry is faithless!

Since our heavenly Father knows that we need to eat, drink and be clothed, let us by faith allow Him to provide them in His time and way. To so act is to rest in God's will and character. In His sovereignty, the Lord knows what we need! Now this does not mean that we have no need to pray about such things from time to time or for a season. It does mean that the whole essence of our relationship with the Father is to be one of total dependence, realizing that often the Father uses these basics of life to build our faith.

There must be a commitment to priorities of a first order, and this means a priority to the kingdom of heaven. Such a commitment takes faith; if we worry, we will not have the time or energy to pursue the heavenly priorities before us in our spheres of influence. The tense of the verb "to seek" in Matthew chapter 6 is present imperative, meaning that it is not only a command for believers but also a continuous command—something we must do continuously every day. We cannot rest on the past laurels of seeking divine priorities or the expectation of seeking those divine priorities, but we must seek His priorities every day in the little things as well as the big issues of life. One cannot seek His will, righteousness and kingdom while worrying at the same time. In essence, if our priorities are divinely right, everything else will fall neatly and uniquely into place. Thus, Matthew 6:33, "Seek first His kingdom and His righteousness, and all these things will be added to you," is a key biblical principle for the whole Christian life.

Those who worry have a fear about the future. They are fearful that the outcome will not be what they wanted or as timely as they needed. This fear can lead to manipulation of people and events (even attempts to manipulate God) to accomplish what they want. This path of worry leads the believer to less dependence upon the Father and less understanding and knowledge of God Himself. Without divine intervention, this path will lead the believer away from living by faith.

On the other hand, the one who walks by faith has a sense of freedom about the future. "Each day has enough trouble of its own." This faithful person prays about those daily troubles to his Father in heaven and about his faith response to those troubles. This person recognizes that today's troubles are the training ground for tomorrow's troubles. A faith response today is a building block for responding by faith tomorrow. That is the divine model, but a response of worry today is a building block for more worry tomorrow. That is the pagan model, and it is just the opposite of the divine model.

Life Response to Biblical Truth
1. Seeing others display faith or hearing others talk about faith is no substitute for walking by faith. Jesus had observed His disciples over a year and had seen but an occasional glimpse

of their walking by faith. It was not the faith-pulse that the Lord was looking for. Paul notes in Colossians 2:6, "Therefore as you have received Christ Jesus the Lord, so walk in Him." We received Christ by faith, and we are to continually walk the same faith. This faith walk is not to be an occasional thing, but living by faith is to permeate all we are and all we do.

When discipling others in Christ, one has to pay attention to the progress of the faith of the disciple. That implies that one needs to be associating with the disciple in as many realms of his or her life as possible so that one can discern whether the faith of the individual is progressing, stagnating or digressing. That discernment is critical in order to know how to teach or speak the Word of God to that individual or body of believers.

2. Most of the time, we ignore or rationalize away the words of our Lord not to lay up for ourselves treasures upon earth. We do this by saying we are not laying up treasures for ourselves as we compare ourselves with those who have many more ostentatious things than we do. When Paul wrote to the Corinthians, he told them that if they "measure themselves by themselves and compare themselves with themselves, they are without understanding" (2 Corinthians 10:12).

Such a comparative mind-set is not wise and is not rooted in faith.

3. Jesus' words in the Sermon on the Mount make it clear that "you cannot serve God and wealth (mammon)." This preoccupation with things or possessions or just stuff is evidenced by an enslavement of the heart to those earthly things, by a vision or focus of the divine that is clouded or blinded by those earthly things and by a usurping of our energy and strength to maintain those worldly things instead of pursuing knowing the Father more intimately.

As an illustration, I must confess that I get preoccupied with certain college football teams. My preoccupation could lead me to searching the Internet for anything positive or negative as to games played, games to be played or recruiting. I could get so preoccupied that I pray about my teams, worry about their winning or losing, and spend endless time speculating the "what ifs" that cannot be changed. On occasion, the Spirit of God has convicted me about this unhealthy preoccupation that has enslaved my heart, has blinded me as to what the divine will is and has devoured my energies foolishly. The service of mammon will choke out the service of God unless the mammon that God has given is placed in a subservient role to God alone.

4. Living by faith has been undermined by legalism, strengths of the flesh and our culture. We are bombarded by messages, consciously and subconsciously, that certain foods and clothing are necessary. However, our Lord says that there is more to life than food and clothing. The feasible set that is in the greater part of this inequality (more to life than food and clothing) is boundless. To be focused on food and clothing or "keeping up with the Joneses" is to miss the bountifulness of God Himself. He is the More-to-Life that we cannot afford to miss and who gives meaning and purpose that His children should all desire. The lilies and grass of the field do not worry about food and clothing, and God is concerned about them. How much more is our Father concerned about us? We each need to ask ourselves under the power of the Holy Spirit if He is our More-to-Life or if we spend too much time and energy on a very narrow subset of things that do not contribute to eternity.

5. The next supernatural feasible set deals with our worth. Our culture blasts us with contradictory messages as to our worth, no matter what our gender, age, education level, athletic prowess, political perspective or ethnic background. As such, these contradictory messages from the world breed inadequacies and inconsistencies in the hearts and minds of God's people. The

consistent message from God's Word, though, is that we are worth more than the birds of the air. We are worth a great deal more because He sent His Son to pay the price for all of our sin. As we see our worth from God's perspective, we are freed to be the individual that He designed us to be. We move into the supernatural feasible set that is boundless instead of the infeasible set that becomes tighter and tighter with narrower views on our worth. Spend time in the Gospels and note the interactions that Jesus had with different people as to gender, race and station in life. They all had incalculable worth and tremendous potential once their faith was placed in "the Lamb of God who takes away the sin of the world" (John 1:29).

6. New reports come out almost weekly that say if an individual eats this food or exercises this way or does something different from the crowd, then he or she will live longer. There is one thing that does not add to the length or the quality of life, and that is worry or anxiety. We worry about things we cannot change; we worry about things that could happen that most likely won't; we worry about the timing of events that may work out for the best; we worry about things that we would not have to worry about if we had just done what we should have done; and we even worry about the worry that we know we should not have. We

live in a culture that is permeated with worry. Our generation has been biased and programmed by the worries of our parents and their parents. The entire context of this worry puts the believer in the infeasible set of not walking by faith. The secret of moving to the supernatural feasible set of nonworry is to focus on the More-to-Life, on Him who is our worth, on His promises from the Scriptures and on knowing our Savior and Lord more intimately each day. Individuals who cultivate that rich personal daily walk with Jesus will walk by faith more and worry less.

7. There are two competing models of living life today in the world: the pagan and the divine. The pagan model is complicated, but the divine model is simplistic and powerful.

First, the divine model is based upon *faith in God* not faith in self as exhibited frequently by worry. Those who walk by faith should have spiritual fruit, walk in obedience to the Scriptures and show a Christlike transformation that should be evident in their lives. Faith is evident not just in words but in deeds. Second, individuals in the divine model *focus on the Father.* Jesus said in John, "No one can come to Me unless the Father who sent Me draws him" (6:44) and, "If you knew Me, you would know My Father also" (8:19). This focus on the Father is critical in understanding His character and the fact that He cannot lie. The strength of this focus bolsters the faith of the individual believer.

A third factor in the divine model has to do with *first-order (heavenly) priorities.* The kingdom of God and God's righteousness must take precedence in our lives. For many of us, this is the difficult one to maintain with the extreme busyness and pace of life. We catch ourselves trying to survive tasks or the activities without having a heavenly perspective. The end result can be no advancement of the kingdom of heaven and no display of heaven's righteousness. The solution is to confess our waywardness and ask God to help us make His priorities our own.

The final portion of the divine model is not having a *fear about the future.* If we have worries about the future, we frequently become impatient with God and begin trying to flesh out solutions on our own—by manipulating people, throwing dollars at the problem and contriving perceived solutions that don't last. When every day is filled with first-order heavenly priorities, we can be in better communion with the Father through the Son, and we will have less worry or hopefully no worry. In addition, our prayer lives will be more in tune to the Father's will, and we will look for the divine solutions to the day's problems. Having first-order heavenly priorities means that worry will not undermine today nor affect tomorrow. The end result of responding by faith today is that a building block is laid to respond by faith tomorrow.

Questions for Reflection

1. Do you sense that you are preoccupied with the things of earth more than the priorities of heaven? For instance, have you been so focused on remodeling the house or redecorating your apartment or just being distracted by busyness at work or in life that you have not gone out of your way to meet a new neighbor or to help someone in need? What should you do?

2. Do you find yourself enslaved to your possessions so that you have little time for God, His Word and ministry to others? If so, what actions should you take?

3. Can you identify the worries in your life at this moment? What are they? Would a close friend identify the same worries? Have these worries clouded your perspective of God in your life? How?

4. Is your worth defined by God, by man or by things that you possess or that possess you? Reflect and pray about that worth.

5. Have you slowly slipped away from the divine model of faith in God, focus on the Father and first-order (heavenly) priorities? Can you identify the time when the slipping away from God began or the events that triggered the slide? List those events or times on a sheet of paper and bring them before God. Talk with God and listen to Him!

6. Do the uncertainties of the times increase your worry about the future, or do they cause you to cling to the Father even more? How is your worry about the future manifested? How should your faith in a sovereign God be manifested?

Chapter 3

Great Faith

Read Matthew 8:5–13 and Luke 7:1–10

The great sermon, the Sermon on the Mount, seems to have been preceded by two miracles of healing on the Sabbath. There was the lame man at the pool of Bethesda in the 5th chapter of John (5:1–15) and the man with the withered hand in three other Gospels (Matthew 12:9–13, Mark 3:1–5, Luke 6:6–11). Mark 3:6–7 reveals that schemes were being hatched by the Pharisees and Herodians to destroy Jesus. His response was to withdraw to the sea with His disciples and great multitudes. Shortly thereafter, He chose the twelve to be with Him and began to teach the disciples on the mountain (Matthew 5:1–2).

In this great sermon, which probably came at the end of Christ's first year of ministry, Jesus addressed the destroyers of faith and noted that the disciples, not just the twelve but the great multitude of disciples (Luke 6:17), had little faith when it came to the basics of life like food, clothing and shelter. From Matthew 8:1, we know that Jesus came down from the mountain with great crowds following Him, and Luke's account in 7:1, 9 tells us that He went to Capernaum, again followed by throngs of people.

All of Jesus' movements were very purposeful! He was fully aware that perceptions of living by faith can be contaminated by the religious establishment, our upbringing, our profession or the times that we live in. He was also aware that deep teaching on the topic of faith does not penetrate into the heart and soul of the believer without some reinforcement and visualization. Four out of nine of Jesus' miracles at this time of His ministry were performed in Capernaum itself while another one or two were accomplished close by. Jesus' return to Capernaum should have been an opportunity for local Jews to respond by faith in light of what they had seen previously, but the great faith response comes from a Gentile who was a Roman soldier and an occupying military leader. What a paradox!

Initial Faith

This centurion, a commander of one hundred foot soldiers (more or less), is the first of four that are mentioned in a favorable light within the New Testament. According to the words of Jesus, there was no one who had such great faith as this centurion in all of Israel. How did this soldier arrive at this faith? Was it instant faith, or was there a process of steps whereby he arrived at this great faith?

The Scriptures recording this event are covered in Matthew 8:5–13 and Luke 7:1–10. A detailed perusal of both passages will find several different types of people mentioned, including a slave (in his home), soldiers (his profession), Jewish elders (his community) and friends (neighbors). It is obvious that the centurion was truly other-oriented as he showed his love toward others by building a synagogue and caring for a lowly slave. A synthesis* of the Matthew and Luke accounts follows:

> [3]And a centurion's slave, who was highly regarded by him, was sick and about to die. When he heard about Jesus, he sent some Jewish elders asking Him to come and save the life of his slave, [1]saying, "Lord, my servant is lying paralyzed at home, fearfully tormented." [3]When they came to Jesus, they earnestly implored Him, saying, "He is worthy for You to grant this to him; for he loves our nation, and it was he who built us our synagogue." [1]Jesus said to him, "I will come and heal him."

Here was a sick slave—paralyzed, about to die and in great pain—who was highly regarded by the

---

* Whenever there is a synthesizing of the Gospel accounts, superscripted numbers are used as follows to indicate the specific Gospel: [1]Matthew, [2]Mark, [3]Luke and [4]John.

centurion. This kind of empathy for another's pain
cannot be faked. And evidently this kind of empathy permeated his whole being—it was not only evident in one realm of his life. Such compassion sug-
gests that this Gentile had come to know the God
of Israel as his Savior. That would help explain his
concern for the synagogue in Capernaum and for
the value of one life, a lowly slave. Even the Jewish
elders sent to fetch Jesus said that he was worthy
for Jesus to act on his behalf. The essence of their assessment was that this centurion was honest, kind,
generous and loving and that such a person desired
this request. Based on merit, this man is certainly
worthy of assistance; but works of the hands do not
merit the attention of God unless the heart of the
individual is obedient to God.

A military leader in occupied lands makes it a
point to stay informed about what is happening in
his sphere of influence. This particular centurion
was surely aware of the miracles that Jesus did in
Capernaum, in the synagogue and in the surrounding area. Most significantly, he probably had first-
hand knowledge of the royal official whose son
was healed by Jesus from a distance as recorded in
John 4:46-54. This royal official felt that Jesus had to
physically be with his son for him to be made well,
but Jesus forced this nobleman's faith to realize
that his son was well when the father believed, no
matter where Jesus was. When Jesus said that He
would come and heal the centurion's slave, the cen-

turion surely knew that the slave would be made well; it was just a matter of time!

The centurion had some initial faith. His request for his slave was highly unusual. In the thirty-five miracles recorded in the Gospels, there are sons, daughters, friends, Gentiles, women, outcasts, the downtrodden and those undervalued in life who are healed, but this is the only healing miracle to do with a slave until the last days of Jesus' ministry (the right ear of the high priest's slave in John 18:10).

Growing Faith

Faith that is vibrant and founded on truth does not stand still and stagnate. Rather, it grows and blossoms even more. This centurion knew that his slave was going to be healed as soon as Jesus got to his home. The synthesized accounts of the 8th chapter of Matthew and the 7th chapter of Luke follow:

> [3]Now Jesus started on His way with them; and when He was not far from the house, the centurion sent friends, saying to Him, "Lord, do not trouble Yourself further, for I am not worthy for You to come under my roof; for this reason I did not even consider myself worthy to come to You, but just say the word, and my servant {boy[1]} will be healed. [1]For I also am a man under authority, with soldiers under me; and I say to this one, 'Go!' and he goes, and to another 'Come!' and he comes, and to my slave, 'Do this!' and he does it."

Two keys to the centurion's faith growing more are found in the "nots": not far and not worthy. When Jesus was "not far" from the home, the centurion sent friends saying that he was "not worthy" for Jesus to come under his roof. The "not far" was probably less than a mile away. Why did it take the centurion this long to come to such a realization when Jesus was almost at his door?

The person wanting to please God will continually be rethinking his or her position or plight in light of the truth being revealed. The truth was that Jesus was coming and was almost at his home, so his slave would be healed; but he, a Gentile, was not fit for Jesus, the Lord of all, to be on his property or in his presence. An understanding of these truths reveals why the centurion was humble before God, why he felt he was unworthy and why he sent friends to ask Jesus for help. In fact, he stopped Jesus from coming any farther since he was so unworthy. James 1:21 rightly captures this situation: "In humility receive the word implanted, which is able to save your souls." It is the soil of humility that nurtures the seeds of truth from heaven.

From this position of humility, the centurion illustrates a good understanding of authority on earth and in heaven. There are those who have authority, and there are those who are under the authority; and each has a divine responsibility. As a centurion with authority, he commanded soldiers and slaves to do what he told them to do. If Jesus, who is from heaven, would just say the word, his servant will be healed. He understood the authority that Jesus had and did not dispute it as the Pharisees and Sadducees continually did. His expectations as to what Jesus could do were in the realm of the impossible. Jesus had said He would come and heal the slave, and He did. His power was not limited by distance or presence. This centurion needed no precedent for his faith to blossom. He didn't have to be boxed in without alternatives to believe, but he could step out in new realms to trust Jesus to do what He said He would do.

Great Faith

Whenever faith in God and His Word is exercised properly, God is pleased. Hebrews 11:6 says, "Without faith it is impossible to please Him." The essence of that pleasure may not be truly evident until the day that God rewards the saints in heaven, but each step of faith is foundational for the next step of faith. The believer whose faith is vibrant and dynamic knows that walking by faith is the only way to please God. There may never be verbal affirmation from the Father, except from the Word, but by faith that is sufficient. Notice the interchange between Jesus and the centurion and the results as recorded in Matthew 8 and Luke 7:

> [1]Now when Jesus heard this, He marveled and said to those who were following, "Truly I say to you, I have not found such great faith with anyone in Israel. I say

to you that many will come from east and west, and recline at the table with Abraham, Isaac and Jacob in the kingdom of heaven; but the sons of the kingdom will be cast out into the outer darkness; in that place there will be weeping and gnashing of teeth." And Jesus said to the centurion, "Go; it shall be done for you as you have believed." And the servant was healed that very moment. [3]When those who had been sent returned to the house, they found the slave in good health.

Jesus marvels when He hears the comments of the centurion that he is not worthy for Jesus to come to his house and that Jesus only needs to say the word for his servant to be healed. The great faith of this centurion, this Gentile, is praised to the multitude, but the lack of faith by those with the promises, the position and the privileges (the Jews and natural heirs, whom Jesus referred to as the sons of the kingdom) are condemned into the outer darkness. As always, entrance into God's kingdom for Jew and Gentile is contingent upon faith in Jesus Christ.

The results of this centurion's great faith are many. First, he got the request that he asked of Jesus, healing of his servant; but most importantly, his faith in Jesus Christ became greater. Second, the servant, who was suffering and dying, was healed and came to know the story about his master and Jesus. This is speculation to a degree, but most likely this servant came to know the Lord as well. Third, the centurion's household would have been affected. Fourth, his friends and the elders from the

synagogue would have been impacted. And finally, the disciples and the multitude following Jesus
should have come to wonder at the great faith of a
Gentile as compared to their own weak faith.

Life Response to Biblical Truth

Many penetrating bullets on faith and living by
faith are communicated by these events surrounding the centurion. Here are some of the applications:

1. For faith to blossom, the heart and eyes of in-
    dividuals must be aware of what God is doing
    around them in their community, profession
    and household. What God is doing will surely
    be missed if one is self-focused and not other-
    focused. And frequently what God is doing is
    not something ostentatious or flamboyant for
    He is in the business of quietly changing lives
    little bit by little bit! The ability to see what God
    is doing requires time in the Scriptures with a
    dependence upon the Holy Spirit to apprehend
    Him, His ways and His words to us. It also re-
    quires a daily walk of obedience in the power
    of the Holy Spirit to see God's hand around us.
    This humble, daily dependence upon Him al-
    lows us to see our world as He does.

2. Great faith needs no precedent! The nobleman
    in John 4:46–54 exhibited faith in Jesus to heal
    his son from a distance, but he was boxed in
    with no other alternatives. He is not commend-

ed for great faith. On the other hand, the centurion stepped out of his box of comfortable faith (and he didn't have to) and asked for the impossible—and he got it, even though he was a Gentile. Both faith responses are to be commended, but the great faith of the centurion was truly more vibrant in light of the results it yielded in other lives.

3. Faith and love could be theoretically mutually exclusive characteristics (1 Corinthians 13:2, 13; James 2), but in Spirit-filled believers they are always coexistent. As such, the individual living by faith seeks the betterment of others. This kind of believer does not see others as the wood, hay and stubble to reach his goal. One way to recognize the lack of faith is to see the carcasses of lives and the vultures hovering over those carcasses in our churches, in other faith-based Christian organizations and on the road of life in our communities. Many of our so-called Christian institutions never do exit interviews of those who leave our midst. If we can continue to ignore how we treated others and avoid biblical change, it is no wonder that we never excel still more in the life of faith. And sadder yet, we really don't know how to impart the truths around such a faith walk to others. The end result is a level of stagnancy in our lives of faith that we may not realize.

4. To live by faith and to excel in faith, one must also understand the implications and the importance of authority and delegation. The centurion truly understood this from his profession as today's Marine does. However, in today's culture, where there is hostility and lack of submission to authority, it is no wonder that great faith is rarely seen. In studying the Gospels, one sees that Jesus taught with authority, displayed authority in casting out demons and calming storms and the seas and granted authority to the twelve disciples. In addition, we see Jesus delegating responsibility to the disciples time after time, such as handing out the bread and fish, collecting the leftovers or getting a colt to ride into Jerusalem. Jesus delegated and expected the delegated task to be done and done correctly. The centurion had the same expectations of those he commanded. This backdrop of authority and delegation is critical to seeing faith blossoming today!

5. Great faith, great humility and great compassion coexist and see a greater God. If our heart clings to treasures other than God, if our mind focuses on things that are not God-ordained and if our will is enslaved to these things or treasures, we will never have great faith in God. If we do not see ourselves as unworthy and Christ as worthy of our all, then we will not have great faith. If we do not see the value of others, especially the

lowest, our faith will not grow, or at most it will grow little.

6. Living by faith impacts not just a select few but all of our spheres of influence. The centurion's step of great faith impacted his household, his employees, his soldiers, his neighbors, his friends, the elders of the synagogue and even his entire community. Maybe the answer to our not-so-powerful witness to our world is turning from disobedience and lack of faith.

7. Matthew 8 and Luke 7 contain some strong admonitions. First, one can be kind, generous and loving (all that the centurion was) and not be in the faith or walking by faith. The checks for this circumstance are whether the individual knows Jesus Christ as their Savior and Lord and whether or not the fruits of the Spirit are being demonstrated in the life and the deeds of the individual. Second, many believers began by faith but are perfecting their faith by the flesh (Galatians 2). This reinforcement comes from Christian entities using merit and performance to evaluate spiritual maturity. Instead, there should be steady discipleship with authority and delegation as well as small groups so that the spiritual status of individuals will be known and nurtured.

8. New believers, outsiders or nonconformists to the in-group, the church or the denomination may be the biggest exercisers of faith. Faith

grows where it is exercised! Look for those who are walking by faith if you want to excel in faith.

9. The life of faith or the daily walk of faith will have revelation (from the Word of God), a relationship (with the God of all), response (doing the will of God completely) and reward (now as God's witness and later).

Questions for Reflection

1. Most of us cannot take steps of faith in many situations without some precedent of God having worked that way previously in our own lives or in the life of another. How does one overcome this need for having a precedent before acting on God's Word or trusting in His person?

2. Living by faith is a daily process or walk. There are opportunities every day to exercise faith in God. If you missed or failed in opportunities that God provided recently, how did you respond to God afterward? What essential interaction between you and God should have occurred? What did you learn about God? What did you learn about yourself?

3. How does a Christian encourage someone to live by faith? How does a parent encourage or exhort a child to walk by faith?

4. On a scale of one to ten, with one being the lowest and ten being the highest, how would you rate your focus on others or compassion toward others? Is your focus toward others with an attitude of per-

sonal favoritism (James 2:1) or is it toward rich and poor alike? How does one assess this honestly?

5. What is the relationship among authority, delegation, humility and faith from this section of Scripture (James chapter 2)? What is God's current proving ground in your life for these things?

6. Since living by faith is to impact all spheres of our life (home, recreation, job, family, neighbors, ministry, use of money and redemption of our time), can you identify at least one opportunity in each sphere in the past two weeks? List them discreetly and prayerfully!

7. Can we depend today upon our faith from last year? How does the passage from Galatians 3:3, "Are you so foolish? Having begun by the Spirit, are you now being perfected by the flesh?" answer this question and challenge us today?

Chapter 4

Faith and the Storms of Life

Read Matthew 8:18, 23–27; Mark 4:35–41
and Luke 8:22–25

All believers will experience some stormy circumstances. Whether these circumstances come one at a time or bunched up, only God knows! Certain bunching of minor circumstances can be just as overwhelming, if not more so, as one major circumstance. These circumstances will surely be stressful events, and five of the top ten stressful events relate to one's spouse: death, divorce, marital separation, marriage and reconciliation. Other top ten stressful events include jail term, death of a close family member, personal injury or illness, being fired from work or even retirement. However, the stormy or stressful event for the disciples recorded in Matthew 8, Mark 4 and Luke 8 was unexpected, unforeseeable, suddenly without warning, without precedence in their experience, life threatening and plain overwhelming. Let's look at their situation and learn!

Since this event is recorded in Matthew, Mark and Luke, one would need to synthesize the words of all three accounts to truly understand the essence of it all. The synthesis follows:

The Tempest
([1]Matthew 8:18–27; [2]Mark 4:35–41; [3]Luke 8:22–25)

> [1]Now when Jesus saw a crowd around Him
>> He gave orders to depart to the other side of the sea.
>
> [2]On that day, when evening came,
>> [3]Jesus and His disciples got into a boat, ([1]His
>> disciples followed Him),
>> [2]He said to them
>> **"Let us go over to the other side [of the lake]."**
> Leaving the crowd, they took Him along with
>> them in the boat, just as He was.
>>> [3]So they launched out
>>> [2]and other boats were with Him.
>
> [3]But as they were sailing along He fell asleep.
> [1]And behold, [3]a fierce gale of wind {a shaking storm}
>>> descended on the lake.
>> [2]And the waves were breaking over the boat
>> so much that the boat was already filling
>>> up. [3]They began to be swamped and to
>>> be in danger.

²Jesus Himself was in the stern, asleep on the cushion;
and they woke Him and said to Him,

> (a) ³"Master, Master, we are perishing!"
> (b) ¹"Save us, Lord; we are perishing!"
> (c) ²"Teacher, do You not care that we are
>   perishing?"

¹*He said to them,*

> (aa) "Why are you afraid, you men of little
>   faith?"
> Then He got up and rebuked the winds and ³the
>   surging waves
> ²and said to the sea, "Hush, be still."
> And the wind died down and it became perfectly calm.

²*And He said to them,*

> (bb) ³"Where is your faith?"
> (cc) ²"Do you still have no faith?"

¹The men were amazed, and ²became very much afraid
>   and said to one another,
> ¹"What kind of a man is this?"
> ³"Who then is this
>   that He commands even the winds and the
>   water and they obey Him?"

Chronologically, this is the thirteenth miracle
of our Lord recorded in the Gospels, and it comes
shortly after the first year of our Lord's ministry. It
is, however, the first visible miracle over creation.
The first miracle of our Lord, turning water into
wine at the wedding in Cana, was not visible to the
naked eye and was a miracle over creation (John
2:1–11). Some of the disciples just saw the results

of this miracle and nothing more. The second miracle over creation was the miraculous catch of fish (Luke 5:1–11), but only some of the disciples were present and what they believed about the catch of fish is not recorded in the Scriptures. Did Jesus create the fish? Did He just know where the fish were? Or did He call the fish to a specific location? Again, the disciples just saw the results of His power. But in this stilling of a storm, all of the disciples are in the midst of the miracle from start to finish. For some reason, until now they had not connected the dots from previous events to understand that the power of this Jesus, the Son of God, was unlimited.

Divine Directive

Jesus had had another full day of ministry, filled with crowds (Matthew 8:18; Mark 4:36), plenty of urgent needs, unexpected twists and little to no time alone. It was time to pull away from it all, but Jesus was tired—probably exhausted (Luke 8:23; Mark 4:38)—and most likely the disciples were tired too. In the midst of this tiredness and frazzle, the Son of God spoke a divine directive to them personally: "Let us go to the other side of the lake." If Jesus said it, there is no perishing possible in His words! In their tiredness, did the disciples not hear these words? There is little chance of that since the Gospel of Mark records this divine directive. In their frazzle, did the disciples not pay close attention to what the Lord said and think through it? That is very likely! Or did the disciples place our Lord's words in the context of everyday familiar conversation and just dismiss them as unimportant chatter? There is no great value in speculating why the Lord's words were not seized upon. However, they were important, and as such there is great value in examining these words.

There are four unique points of information in this divine directive: departure, direction, destination and a duo. As to departure, our Lord said, "Let us go." There was no way they could continue to give of themselves without jeopardizing their well-being. They were all very tired and needed a change. The direction that they were to take was to the "other side of the lake." This specific direction was directed at the disciples and no one else. The third ingredient of the divine directive was a destination, "the other side of the lake." The final aspect of Jesus' words was that the disciples were not departing in a direction of life or ministry or toward a destination alone but in duo, meaning Jesus and the individual.

Many commands of Scripture will have these same four bits of information. Sometimes, there is no departure in a direction but rather a waiting. Other times the destination is not clear, but we can be sure that obedience to the commands of Scripture always leads to the destination of being more like Christ. And finally, whatever our Lord commands us to do or speaks personally to us and our circumstances is never expected to be done alone but with Him, in the power of the Holy Spirit!

Before leaving our discussion of this divine directive, it is important to note that these words were not delivered to the people in the other boats (Mark 4:36) that were following with them. These words were specifically addressed to the disciples in the one boat. The people in the other boats could not claim these words as applying to them. If the individual believer today can say, as Samuel did in 1 Samuel 3:10, "Speak, for Your servant is listening," then there will be a word from the Lord specific to that believer.

Distress

"God is our refuge and strength, abundantly available for help in tight places. Therefore we will not fear" (Psalm 46:1–2).* The disciples were assuredly in a tight place, a small boat in a fierce storm. Their distress was truly magnified by the unexpectedness of the storm, the abruptness of it, the frightening appearance of it and the life-threatening character of it. In addition, darkness had set in (things always look worse in the dark), there was a fierce gale of wind—basically a hurricane gale—and the boat was filling up and ready to be swamped. Surely the situation was perilous!

On top of all this, this storm struck at their strength and at their profession—at least four of the

---

* Literal translation of this verse.

disciples were professional fishermen. They had seen many storms, but this one was different. All of their sailing skills and years of experience were of no help. All self-efforts for self-deliverance were of no use. The disciples were hemmed in or cornered, physically and emotionally. Years ago, Catherine Marshall wrote of such a situation after the death of her husband, Peter:

> Gradually I had come to recognize this hemming-in process as one of God's most loving and effective devices for teaching us that He is gloriously adequate for our problems . . . these kinds of crises bring us face to face with our inadequacy and our inadequacy in turn leads us to the inexhaustible sufficiency of God.[1]

Was the response of the disciples in this storm one of faith? No, instead of a faith response, there was fear, panic, selfishness (no concern for the people in the other boats) and forgetfulness of the divine directive, "Let us go to the other side of the lake." To forget or not even to know the words of our Savior certainly is the underlying root cause of our fear or panic. Visualize the picture of some of the disciples waking the Lord, who was asleep in the stern of the boat, with the rapid fire of the following comments and one question: "[3]Master, Master, we are perishing! [1]Save us, Lord; we are perishing! [2]Teacher, do You not care that we are perishing?" Notice the emphasis on "we are perishing." There is no concern for the people in the other boats. The last question,

"Do You not care . . ." defames God and His character. God's power for our storms, His knowledge of them and His sovereignty and love in allowing them are all part of the divine plan in helping us progress in the life of faith and obedience. Without storms, there would never be supernatural strength and dependence developed in our lives.

Deliverance

The Creator of the heavens and the earth knows (a) what to do and (b) when to act. The Sovereign One is not surprised by the storms. He knew before time began that they would come our way and what He would do in each if we would but let Him. However, His time to act in the storm is His, not ours. We all are guilty of trying to dictate what God should do and when to do it when going through these storms of life, but the what to do and the when to do are His prerogative! That is the tension in the life of faith.

Notice that the Omnipotent One arose and rebuked the wind and the surging waves. The word used here for "rebuke" is used elsewhere of rebuking demons. It is very likely that the origin of this storm was Satan himself (Job 1:19) with an idea to wipe out Jesus and His key followers once and for all. But the Omniscient One is never surprised by the methods of the evil one. When Jesus does what He plans to do and when He plans to do it, it is always completely sufficient. He spoke to the wind and the waves. He spoke to the cause of the storm (the wind) and the results of the storm (the waves). The end result was that "it became perfectly calm."

Our Creator, our Redeemer and our Friend does the same today ("Jesus Christ is the same yesterday and today and forever" Hebrews 13:8). He can take any storm that you or I may be going through and calm the causes of the storm as well as the results of the storm. When He is in the middle of the storm and we allow Him to work and act in His way and in His time, there is a perfect calmness that occurs in our circumstances and hearts.

Didactic or an Instructive Interchange

"Why are you afraid, you men of little faith?" (Matthew 8:26). "Where is your faith?" (Luke 8:25). "Do you still have no faith?" (Mark 4:40). These three questions from the three different Gospels have always troubled me and have been irreconcilable until recently. The first question about men of little faith is more understandable in the context of faith in Matthew. In the Sermon on the Mount, our Lord addresses worry or anxiety about food, clothing and life to the disciples. He calls them, "You of little faith" (Matthew 6:30).

Shortly, after the Sermon on the Mount, the Lord is amazed at the great faith the centurion, a Gentile, displayed. Another Gentile, a Canaanite woman, is commended for her great faith (Matthew 15:28). However, there are three more references to little faith, and they all revolve around the twelve disciples: Peter, walking on the water (Matthew 14:31), is lightly chided for his little faith; the disciples, forgetting to bring bread (Matthew 16:8), are also said to be men of little faith; and lastly, the failure to cast a demon out of a father's son is tied to the small faith of the disciples (Matthew 17:20). Thus, the first question about the timidity of these men of little faith addresses where the faith of the disciples was overall. It was little, as recorded throughout the Gospel of Matthew.

The second query from our Lord as to "Where is your faith?" is a pointed question to the disciples as to whether or not they are exercising faith in the present crisis. "Where is your faith?" is the type of question the Lord asks us sometimes and is one requiring much meditation as prompted by the Holy Spirit. It is a question that needs to be asked of us several times in the storms of our lives until we have an accurate and truthful assessment of the current state of our faith.

The third question, "How is it that you have no faith?" is the Lord's current assessment of the disciples' faith in this storm. They have displayed no faith! Their overall faith is little, but their faith in the current situation is nonexistent. Over the years, I have had the privilege to disciple many men, and sometimes those men have not exercised faith in some very critical situations. With fear and trembling and under the prompting of the Holy Spirit,

I have spoken individually to a few of these men noting a lack of faith being exercised. For the most part, these men have understood that the assessment was of their faith in the current circumstance, not of their overall faith.

Dazzled Disciples

The response of the disciples to the storm, the display of God's power over creation led to much fear and reverence, along with unanswered questions. "What kind of a man is this?" (Matthew 8:27). "Who then is this, that He commands even the winds and the water, and they obey Him?" (Luke 8:25). The disciples are beginning to realize that this Jesus is far greater than they ever imagined. His control over sickness, demons, God's creation and the storms of our lives is beyond our human frailty to grasp; but by faith, it all makes sense! May God ask us all, when it is appropriate, "Where is your faith?"

Life Response to Biblical Truth

1. Storms are an inevitable part of life, and frequently they cannot be avoided or navigated around. These storms are sovereignly permitted and specifically designed to move us, as individual believers, closer to God and His Word. The big question for each of us is how we will or should respond in the storms.

2. Precursory events are sometimes critical in understanding the storms allowed to come our way. Some reflection, meditation and prayer may be necessary—not massive introspection but a searching of our hearts and minds by the Spirit of God. Questions to ponder might be: (a) "What was God's Word to me prior to the storm?"(b) "Where was I going?" and (c) "Why was I going in that direction?"

3. The no-faith response in a storm is certainly not the way for believers, but how does one recognize that he or she is not responding by faith? From these three Gospel accounts, the litmus test for not responding by faith is threefold. First, what is my concern for others and their welfare? Second, what focus do I have on Jesus' words? And third, has fear or panic set in? Fear and faith cannot coexist in storms!

4. We need others to challenge or help us assess where our faith is both overall, in past years and recently. This is important because we are sheep, not lone rangers. We are commanded to love one another, to build up one another, to comfort one another, to pray for one another, to admonish one another and more. Obedience to these "one another" commands does not take place in a vacuum but in the context of rich relationships with other believers.

5. We need to realize that God can calm the storm immediately, but frequently that is not His choice if His goal is to grow our faith and dependence.

6. Storms will not only stimulate our faith in God and His Word, but also they will provide new or refreshed perspectives of His person, His power and His presence. These storms, if embraced as allowed by God, can even enrich and empower our worship of the Lord.

7. Feelings and perceptions such as loneliness, being overwhelmed, seeming incapable and fear are real from the human side of the equation. But from the divine side, the Lord is ever with us so we are not alone, God is never swamped and nothing is beyond His ability to handle or correct.

8. Storms strike in the area of strengths. The most difficult lesson for the saint to learn is to walk by faith in areas of his or her strength. The tendency to exercise faith in our areas of weakness is high, but Jesus is interested in having first place in every area of life (Colossians 1:17–18).

9. God is never asleep during the storms of our lives. He cares intensely; but the storm is necessary for our faith to grow, to move us out of stagnancy or comfort zones and to equip us to minister to others who will also pass this way.

10. Scripture continually admonishes us to "take care how you listen." The next time the Lord speaks to us from the Scriptures, may we ask: What does it say about my departure, my direction and my destination? We can always be confident that He will be with us and will enable us to be obedient to the command if we only trust Him.

Questions for Reflection

1. It was noted that storms or tight places are inevitable parts of life. Remember or reflect on God's faithfulness in past storms or tight places. How is your current difficult or impossible situation unlike what you experienced before? What was your perspective of God at the end of the previous tight place or storm? What is your perspective now?

2. These unexpected and uncontrollable storms bring us face to face with our own inadequacies in our strengths and weaknesses, much like the fishermen whose expertise wasn't good enough in the storm. What have been your responses in the past to such situations? Verbally? Emotionally? Spiritually? Toward others? Toward God's Word?

3. As a result of past storms, what has been the impact on your faith in God and His Word?

4. While in the storm or after it, what kinds of opportunities did God provide to comfort others? Would your compassion or empathy toward others have been the same without the storm? Comment on how God expanded the experience for good!

5. Did God seem to be asleep or distant while in your storm? How did this perception affect you? With anger at Him? With questions of why? With overwhelming loneliness or what?

6. Many times we have not cultivated the habit of listening to God as that gentle, quiet voice. As a result, these storms are necessary to get us to realign our focus on God. What has been the aftermath impact of such storms on your relationship with God?

7. Do you have friends who would ask you where your faith is in such storms or tight places? Do you have deep relationships with others in such a way that you could ask them the same query? What is the implication of these two questions?

Chapter 5

Peter's Walking on the Water or Peter's Twelve Steps of Faith and Failure

Read Matthew 14:22–33; Mark 6:45–52;
John 6:1–21

In the storm on the sea, all of the disciples had their faith tested. While there was some measure of corporate and corporeal testing in the boat ride (Matthew 14:22–33; Mark 6:45–52), the prime focus is on one individual's faith: Peter's. This particular event, the nineteenth miracle of Christ recorded in the Gospels, quickly follows the feeding of the five thousand (Matthew 14:13–21; Mark 6:30–44; Luke 9:10–17; John 6:1–14). What happens during the feeding of the five thousand is critical to understanding the events that follow. Thus, before synthesizing the Gospel accounts surrounding Peter, we must take a quick look at the precursory events.

Precursory Events at Feeding of the Five Thousand

John 6:2 tells us that "a large crowd followed Him, because they saw the signs which He was performing on those who were sick." Mark 6:34 says, "He felt compassion for them because they were like sheep without a shepherd." In this situation of great need, Jesus tested the disciples "for He Himself knew what He was intending to do" (John 6:6). The Gospels of Matthew, Mark and Luke all indicate that Jesus wanted the disciples to give the people something to eat; but John's account, pieced together with the other Gospels, gives a different picture. There were directed questions and diverse responses, but Jesus was looking for a response of faith.

> Therefore Jesus, lifting up His eyes and seeing that a large crowd was coming to Him, said to Philip, "Where are we to buy bread, so that these may eat?" This He was saying to test him, for He Himself knew what He was intending to do. Philip answered Him, "Two hundred denarii worth of bread is not sufficient for them, for everyone to receive a little." One of His disciples, Andrew, Simon Peter's brother, said to Him, "There is a lad here who has five barley loaves and two fish, but what are these for so many people?" (John 6:5–9)

Reply of figures and not faith

Philip correctly estimated that it would take seven months' wages to give just a little to each individual in the crowd. Philip was from the area of Bethsaida (John 1:44) so he should have known about available resources and options. His response is like the response of the statistician, the engineer or the mathematically inclined individual who uses numbers, models and very systematic but linear thinking to estimate needs or future possibilities. There is nothing wrong with that tendency and thinking (Luke 14:28–32), but figures or numbers should not drive our faith. In fact, our faith is based on one Figure, Jesus Christ!

Reply of food not faith

Andrew knew what food was available, merely five barley loaves and two sardine-type fish. His response was that of an accountant who assessed the resources and found them inadequate. Accountants must know the debits and credits for a business so that they can balance the books. If the books don't balance, other options may be necessary. But this assessment by Andrew left out the most important resource of all, the Creator of the heavens and the earth, the omnipotent One. Without God, the correct assessment of resources always falls short!

Reply of each foraging for own food

The Gospel of Luke says that the twelve disciples came to Jesus suggesting that He "send the crowd away, that they may go into the surrounding villages and countryside and find lodging and get something to eat; for here we are in a desolate place" (Luke 9:12). This could be the response of the rugged survivalist that everyone is on his own to meet his own needs. Let the individual depend upon personal resourcefulness, whom he knows, what he has, what he can get, whom he can manipulate and so on. On the other hand, the corporate thinking of the twelve could have been an attempt to move the problem from sight. However, these five thousand men (plus all the women and children) had been under Jesus' teaching (Mark 6:34) so there was a responsibility to meet their needs. Again, the faithless response does not see human needs with eyes of compassion. The faithful response knows that Jesus is compassionate and does meet needs of individuals and groups.

Jesus seeking a reply of faith

In an attempt to draw the disciples out to respond by faith, Jesus told them, "They do not need to go away; you give them something to eat!" (Matthew 14:16). As our Savior does so well, He put the onus or the burden back on them so that they would turn to Him in their inability and weakness and might see Him as sufficient for every need and situation. But that response of faith did not occur!

Disciples' reply of compromise

From Luke 9:13, we know that the last response of the disciples was to combine what food they had (five loaves and two fish) with money to buy from the local economy what they might need. This compromising response is typical of the diplomatic perspective, but it is also inadequate because it leaves out the sufficient One!

Jesus' reply of faith and action

The essence of this interchange was to show that Jesus was trying to help the disciples to respond by faith, but four failures at seeing things from the divine perspective forced Jesus to move on and quickly do what needed to be done. He would return to these issues later as He does with Peter walking on the water. However, Jesus subtly continues teaching and illustrating the essences of faith in feeding the five thousand. He does this in the organization of the people, the distribution of the bread and fish and the collection of the leftovers.

The organization structure was designed to help the disciples understand living by faith. The crowd was five thousand men in size (Luke 9:14), but considering women and children, a statistician's estimate of crowd size would be anywhere from twelve to twenty thousand people. The crowd was organized into groups of hundreds and fifties, according to Mark 6:40, or about fifty each according to Luke 9:14. Assuming the average group size of men was seventy-five (fifty plus one hundred divided by two), this yields about sixty-seven groups. But if one considers the words of Luke, "about fifty," there might be some additional groups. If we suppose that there were about seventy-two such groups, this would mean that each disciple would have taken food from Jesus' hand at least six different times (seventy-two divided by twelve equals six).

This organization structure provides keys to faith in the distribution process of the food. When one considers that each group had about seventy-five men and another one hundred and fifty women and children (assuming fifteen thousand people in total), there would have been repeated trips back to Jesus for bread and fish. The Luke account says that Jesus "kept giving them to the disciples to set before the people" (9:16). Time after time, the disciples ran out of bread and fish, but on returning to Jesus their supply was replenished. Does not this organizational and distributional structure show the dependence that the disciples had on the Lord?

The process for the collection of the leftovers highlighted the following facts: What Jesus provides is always sufficient (John 6:11), what He gives is always satisfying (Luke 9:17) and what He offers is always superabundant (John 6:13). Seeing that kind of sufficiency, satisfaction and superabundance should have helped the disciples understand the earlier faith interchange, but we know from Mark that "they had not gained any insight from the incident of the loaves" (6:52).

Protecting the Disciples

Whenever God's children fail in the life of faith after repeated testing and prompting, our Lord knows how weak we are, how susceptible to temptation and how prone to make unwise decisions we are. Piecing together the Gospels of Matthew 14:22–23, Mark 6:45–46 and John 6:14–15, we have the following account (synthesized):

> [4]Therefore when the people saw the sign which He had performed, they said, "This is truly the Prophet who is to come into the world." So Jesus, perceiving that they were intending to come and take Him by force to make Him king, [2] made His disciples get into the boat and go ahead of Him to the other side to Bethsaida, while He Himself was sending the crowd away. After bidding them farewell, He left for the mountain [1]by Himself to pray; and when it was evening, He was there alone.

Jesus knows all men, and He knows what is in the heart of men. Becoming king was not in the divine plan, no matter what the multitude thought. The divine order required suffering, death and resurrection; and yet there was no way to convince the crowds of that at this time. Jesus also knew the frailty of the disciples in understanding the concepts of walking by faith and that there is a time for every event under the sun. The time for kings and kingdoms was not then so the first step of protection was when Jesus sent the disciples away to the boat. He was trying to shield them from this unbiblical or earthly thinking. The second step of protection was that He personally dismissed the crowds, trying to prevent the avalanche of popular opinion from gaining any speed and affecting the divine plan. The third step of protection, and probably the most important, was that He withdrew to a lonely place to pray by Himself. His prayers certainly covered His disciples' exposure to king-and-kingdom thinking, their stumbles in the life of faith, the crowd's reach for quick fixes and His need for strength and resolve to hold the course.

The essence of this protection is not in the same realm as a shepherd physically protecting his sheep, but rather protection of the mind/heart/soul of believers in their faith in the Sovereign One and His word. Jesus' prayers were a rich dialogue of listening and talking with the Father.

Powerful Realities

[4]Now when evening came, His disciples went down to the sea, and after getting into a boat, they started to cross the sea to Capernaum. It had already become dark, and Jesus had not yet come to them. [1]But the boat was already a long distance [or many stadia where one stadia was about two hundred yards] from the land, battered by the waves, for the wind was contrary. [4]The sea began to be stirred up because a strong wind was blowing. [2]Seeing them straining at the oars, for the

wind was against them ⁴[they had rowed about three or four miles], ²at about the fourth watch of the night He came to them, walking on the sea; and He intended to pass by them.

¹When the disciples saw Him walking on the sea ⁴and drawing near to the boat, ¹they were terrified, and said, ¹"It is a ghost!" And they cried out in fear. ²For they all saw Him and were terrified. ¹But immediately Jesus spoke to them, saying, "Take courage, it is I; do not be afraid." (Matthew 14:22–27; Mark 6:47–50; John 6:16–21)

The realities of our circumstances can be overwhelming sometimes, and that surely was the case with the disciples. It was dark, and they were alone on the water. They had probably left Jesus at the first watch (6 to 9 p.m.), and Jesus came to them at the fourth watch (3 to 6 a.m.). The end result was that they had been rowing six to twelve hours and were obviously exhausted. Their rowing had been against contrary winds, and they had not reached their destination. Thus, they would have been emotionally and physically spent from the day's events. That condition leaves one very fearful of unusual things seen or encountered. They thought they were seeing ghosts, and all of the disciples were gripped with fear.

Jesus had intended to pass the disciples by; but when He realized the environment of fear, He spoke the Word of God to allay that fear. The words spoken by the Living Word gave a solution to their fearful dilemma because the heart encompassed by fear cannot respond by faith. First, Jesus told them to "take courage" or be of good cheer. Another way to say this is to "put on courage." Second, He said, "It is I" or the "I am" is here. In other words, the person of God is here right now in the midst of your troubling, straining, dark circumstances. And then the Lord said, "Do not be afraid" or "Put off the fear" that has gripped your being and heart. These words also apply to any such troubling, difficult and dark circumstances that each of us may be going through. Put off the old man and all of his corrupted perspectives, and put on the new man, "which in the likeness of God has been created in righteousness and holiness of the truth" (Ephesians 4:24). The person of God in the Holy Spirit is available to every believer. We need to realize God's presence and power are always there to dispel the fears that destroy living by faith.

Peter's Steps of Faith

The interchange between Peter and our Lord is rich in truth and application, and it is critical to understand it if we are going to progress in the life of faith. The dialogue is unique to the Gospel of Matthew:

> But immediately Jesus spoke to them, saying, "Take courage, it is I; do not be afraid." Peter said to Him, "Lord, if it is You, command me to come to You on the water." And He said, "Come!" And Peter got out of the boat, and walked on the water and came toward

Jesus. But seeing the wind, he became frightened, and beginning to sink, he cried out, "Lord, save me!" Immediately Jesus stretched out His hand and took hold of him, and said to him, "You of little faith, why did you doubt?" When they got into the boat, the wind stopped. (Matthew 14:27–32)

Within this short interchange between our Lord and Peter, there are twelve steps or circumstances that need to be noted.

1. **The query of the Lord.** Evidently, Peter recognized the Lord's voice since the phrase "Lord, if it is you" has an assumed reality in the Greek language of the New Testament. We too, when we hear the Lord's voice today, should query Him for directions as to how to proceed. Peter's petition has boldness, "Command me to come to You on the water." It is this kind of boldness or confidence that believers need today, but sadly most are not familiar enough with the voice of their Savior. "Beloved, if our heart does not condemn us, we have confidence before God; and whatever we ask we receive from Him, because we keep His commandments and do the things that are pleasing in His sight" (1 John 3:21–22).

2. **The Lord's answer.** What makes the Lord's answer remarkable is its simplicity—one word, a command: "Come!" There is no nagging to come or repetition of the command. There is just a simple command to Peter and only Peter.

3. **Peter got out of the boat.** Peter heard the Lord's answer and acted. He ignored his comfort zone, his status quo, his tiredness and all of the excuses he could have made and stepped out in faith. That is faith in action.

4. **He walked on water.** Peter's faith is evident as he walks on water. How many steps he took toward Jesus are not recorded in Scripture, but surely ten or more.*

5. **He walked toward Jesus.** The walk of faith begun by Peter was toward Jesus, which is to be commended. He didn't get out of the boat and go his own merry way, but his exit out of the boat was toward Jesus with his eyes on Him.

6. **Seeing the wind.** The steps of faith that we make toward Jesus should always be commended. But Peter took his eyes off Jesus and focused on the wind and the tumultuous waves (the results of the wind). In certain God-ordained life-ven-

---

* My conclusion on this is quite complicated, but here it goes from multiple issues. First, commercial fishermen typically have a gaff hook in the boat that can range from 3 to 12 feet (1 to 4 steps) plus in length to pull fish in. Peter was definitely beyond that reach. Second, the disciples saw Jesus walking by but couldn't recognize him. That probably puts Jesus at 30 to 50 yards away. Third, when Peter began to sink, the Scriptures say that immediately Jesus stretched out His hand and took hold of him. With all of that being said, my best statistical estimate of distance covered was no less than 10 yards or 10 steps but most likely 20 or 30 steps since he was close to Jesus. The understanding of this is a rich application for walking by faith!

tures, we believers start well but slowly fix our eyes on the problems and difficulties caused by the winds of our circumstances. Such a momentary fixation can easily be corrected by looking back to Jesus.

7. **Peter began to sink.** The wrong fixation of our spiritual eyes leads to that sinking feeling, and the more intensely our eyes are focused on the wrong things, the faster the sinking seems to occur. In this case, one gets the impression that the sinking was not immediate but gradual. This sinking of Peter would become ammunition for nonbelievers and even some believers to make a big deal out of his failure in the life of faith.

8. **His cry to the Lord.** Peter sinks in the water and cries to the Lord for help. His call is short but sufficient. Peter recognizes from where his help is to come so his failure is quickly followed by an act of faith.

9. **The timeliness of the answer.** Jesus did not wait until things got worse. The Scriptures record that "immediately Jesus stretched out His hand." In response to Peter's cry, the Lord responded, showing that there is always timeliness to Jesus' answer to a request for help.

10. **In the hand of Jesus.** Jesus takes hold of Peter and pulls him up. Once He delivers him from the waves and wind, He reprimands him for his

littleness of faith. Our tendency might be to lecture Peter about the failure and its causes before getting involved in the deliverance. Jesus' approach focuses more on the individual's well-being!

11. **They walked back together.** There is not much said in the Scriptures here, except that "they got into the boat." Once Jesus caught hold of Peter, they assuredly walked back to the boat with Jesus holding Peter's hand the whole way. Peter had exercised faith in stepping out of the boat and walking toward Jesus, and he exercised faith again in asking the Master for help. But Jesus understands men whose faith is frail. Time for reflection and refocus on the Savior and His word are critical for future success in the arena of the last failure.

12. **The wind stopped.** Notice that the winds didn't stop until Jesus and Peter were back in the boat. Even today, when we ask in faith, the trials and difficulties don't always end; but they are an opportunity for us to walk hand in hand with our Savior through them. That fellowship with the Savior is something to be cherished in today's topsy-turvy world.

Prologue to the Miracle

⁴So they were willing to receive Him into the boat. ²They were utterly astonished, for they had not gained any insight from the incident of the loaves, but their

heart was hardened. ¹And those who were in the boat worshiped Him, saying, "You are certainly God's Son!" ⁴And immediately the boat was at the land to which they were going. (Matthew 14:33, Mark 6:51–52, John 6:21)

With all of the miraculous events—Jesus walking on the water, Peter walking on the water, the rescuing of Peter, the walk back to the boat by Jesus and Peter and the stopping of the winds—the disciples were willing to receive Jesus into the boat. Would the faith of the disciples be enlarged by all of the miracles they just saw? Probably not! From the Gospel of Mark (6:52–53) we see their response was one of astonishment, but they had not gained any insight from the incidence of the feeding of the five thousand just prior. The Mark account says that they did not understand since their hearts were hardened—and hardened hearts cannot respond by faith. The fact that Peter took the steps of faith he did in this environment of unbelief is really amazing.

Finally, those in the boat worshipped Him and voiced their recognition of Him as God's Son; but if the events that follow are any indication, it is very likely that their faith had not progressed. After all of this, the boat was immediately at land, which was another small miracle to be seen by the eyes of faith.

Life Response to Biblical Truth

While hundreds of biblical principles could be drawn from this text, here are five of the main ones:

1. The didactic interchange with the disciples before the feeding of the five thousand, the distribution of the food and the retrieval of the
   leftovers by the disciples, Jesus' and Peter's
   walking on the water and the accompanying
   miracles and teaching were all efforts of a loving Father and Son trying to help the children
   of God progress in the life of faith. These efforts weren't wasted, for God does not waste
   time or experiences. He uses everything to
   accomplish His purposes even if the heart is
   hardened. The culmination of these efforts may
   not have shown up until after the death and
   resurrection of Christ, but surely the disciples
   would have chided themselves for such blindness and lack of dependence upon the Lord.

2. All believers have natural and spiritual strengths
   whether it is the ability to analyze data, collect
   resources, forage for solutions or work out compromises. These may be strong suits for some
   while other believers may have different ones.
   However, no Christian can trust in his natural
   or spiritual strengths. That trust must be in Jesus and Jesus alone. All strengths and weaknesses have been given to us by God, but they
   are never to be a substitute for living by faith
   or trusting in Him. We should ask ourselves
   if we always depend on God and not on our
   strengths. If not, we need to pray that we will.

3. Hardness of heart or prolonged unbelief results in greater hardness of heart. That kind of heart is far removed from the sphere of faith. The Word of God is necessary to break the encasement of fear that is choking out the heart. Even today, we need to hear the words of the Apostle Paul, "You lay aside the old self, which is being corrupted in accordance with the lusts of deceit . . . and put on the new self, which in the likeness of God has been created in righteousness and holiness of the truth" (Ephesians 4:22–24). Jesus' words to the disciples pointed out that it is not possible to put off the old and put on the new without divine empowerment. Today, that empowerment comes from the Holy Spirit, using the sword of the Spirit—the Word of God. One of the dilemmas occurring today in the body of Christ is that the teaching of the Word of God is minimized and that illustrations, philosophies of men and antidotes are maximized. The results are fleshly perspectives rather than biblical perspectives. The Bible "is living and active and sharper than any two-edged sword, and piercing as far as the division of soul and spirit, of both joints and marrow, and able to judge the thoughts and intentions of the heart" (Hebrews 4:12). It is the Word of God that came to those disciples in the boat that dark night after a very long and draining day. It is the Word of God that must also come to us.

4. To progress in the life of faith, we must ask these questions: Do we hear or recognize the voice of the Lord? Does the Lord have to repeat what He said, or can He say it simply once and we obey? Are we willing to get out of the boat and go in the direction the Lord has indicated? Are we willing to walk where no one has walked before? Are we willing to walk toward Jesus only, or are we sidetracked by walking toward what men want?

5. On the negative side, when we take our eyes off of Jesus, we can be guaranteed that we will sink. Sometimes that sinking is very slow or so slow that we don't realize that Jesus is not our total focus any longer. When the sinking comes quickly, we frequently make the correct correlations. But when it is slow, the depravity of the human heart makes other excuses or rationalizations for our failure. We need to remember that on occasion we all take our eyes off the Lord. What is extremely refreshing is that He sees us, He is always present with us and He is waiting for us to cry out to Him. When we do, His answer is always timely. And when He answers, He grasps us since we don't really have the means or strength to hold onto Him. Jesus will walk with us back to where we need to be. What a Savior!

Questions for Reflection

1. We put faith in figures, bank accounts, abilities, God-given resources, previous successes, who we know and more, but has your faith been in God alone over the past six months? Spend some time alone with God on this very issue, asking Him to search your heart and reveal the deceptions or realities.

2. The Scriptures note that the disciples had not gained any insight from the incident of loaves or the storm on the sea (Mark 6:52). Do you have intimate friends or people in your life who hold you accountable to walk by faith? How would you respond to such a statement that you had not learned anything from the previous faith-exhorting event?

3. We have all had times where we were physically and/or emotionally depleted so much that we did not hear or recognize the Lord's voice. What would have provided critical help in recognizing and obeying the Lord's voice? What are the safeguards that you could put in place?

4. The Lord God does not waste experiences that pre-cede and follow a faith-building event. As such, what does that imply that we must do to see His hand and His ways in life?

5. God frequently asks us to step out of our comfort zone in new and unique ways for which there are no precedents. Can you recount such ways in your life that might be an encouragement to someone else and his or her faith?

6. Whenever we take our eyes off Jesus, we will sink, sometimes very slowly and sometimes rapidly. Can you recount such events and what you learned when the category of sinking was very slow versus very fast?

7. It is a beautiful reassurance that God protects His children, knowing their frailty and purposely not testing them beyond what they are able to handle. Reflect on God's faithfulness in protecting your faith over the past three months. What value do you at-tach to such acts from God?

Chapter 6

Faith and Prayer

Read Matthew 15:21–28 and Mark 7:24–30

Thus far, much of the discussion about faith has centered on the disciples and Jesus. However, living by faith is not just for those in leadership; it is for everyone in the body of Christ. This is exhibited by a centurion asking for Jesus to heal his servant (Matthew 8:5–13, Luke 7:1–10), by a woman with an issue of blood (Matthew 9:20–22, Mark 5:25–34, Luke 8:43–48), by a mother seeking healing of a daughter (Matthew 15:21–28, Mark 7:24–30) and by a father desiring deliverance for a demon-possessed son (Matthew 17:14–21, Mark 9:14–29, Luke 9:37–42). No matter what our station in life or our place in the body of Christ, we are to walk by faith—"Therefore as you have received Christ Jesus the Lord, so walk in Him" (Colossians 2:6). Living by faith is not optional; it is indispensable for every believer!

The events surrounding this Gentile mother's interaction with Jesus are recorded only in the Gospels of Matthew (15:21–28) and Mark (7:24–30). Johnston Cheney gives some understanding to the timing of this event about faith:

> When the religious leaders were outraged at Jesus' zeal in cleansing the temple, He withdrew to the country districts. When jealousy developed with respect to His relation to John the Baptist, He withdrew to Galilee. When His hometown rejected Him, He withdrew to a friendlier city. When His second visit at Jerusalem met rejection, He withdrew again to Galilee. And when at the beginning of the third year, His adopted city of Capernaum rejected Him, He withdrew to Gentile regions of Palestine. In a later visit to Jerusalem to display His resurrection power in the raising of Lazarus He again withdrew to outlying areas to foil a plot to destroy Him. In the face of this general rejection . . . He would withdraw from the entire world of men.[1]

The hardness of heart, the conflict and the blindness of people that Jesus experienced in Jerusalem, in Capernaum and in general ministry necessitated that He on occasion withdraw. There is a time for everything (Ecclesiastes 3:1–8)—to press on and to withdraw, and this was one of those times to draw back to the Gentile regions:

> [1]Jesus went away from there, and withdrew into the district of Tyre and Sidon, [2]to the region of Tyre. And when He had entered a house, He wanted no one to know of it, yet He could not escape notice (Matthew 15:21; Mark 7:24).

Jesus withdrew to this Gentile region, trying to avoid attention. During this time, we see a beautiful, blossoming display of faith as it is drawn out by our Savior and Lord. What is exciting about the interchange between Jesus and the Gentile woman (Mark 7:25–30) is that our God uses some of the same methods to help our faith blossom today.

Petitions That Progress

Many times when we pray we get in a rut in our petitions by repeating the same thing time after time. We even expect to be heard because of our repetition. Jesus said in Matthew 6:7, "When you are praying, do not use meaningless repetition as the Gentiles do, for they suppose that they will be heard for their many words." This Gentile woman does not stay in the repetitive mold very long. There is progression in her perspectives of who Jesus is and how to lay hold of His words by faith.

> [2]But after hearing of Him, [1]a Canaanite woman from that region came out, [2]whose little daughter had an unclean spirit, immediately came and fell at His feet. Now the woman was a Gentile, of the Syrophoenician race [1]and began to cry out, saying, "Have mercy on me, Lord, Son of David; my daughter is cruelly demon-possessed."

²And she kept asking Him to cast the demon out of her daughter, ¹but He did not answer her a word. (Matthew 15:21–23; Mark 7:25–26)

Three words are used to describe this woman: *Gentile*, showing her religious background; *Syrophoenician*, detailing her geographic roots; and *Canaanite*, showing her ancestry (an ancestry that was cursed). The Scriptures also say her petition was not for herself but for her little daughter, who had an unclean spirit. The Gospel of Mark records that her little daughter was "cruelly demon-possessed," implying that her young daughter was very sick indeed.

What is most interesting about this woman's petition for her daughter is the progression or journey that her prayers take. In this case, there are four petitions, but only the last petition is biblically proper. May we learn from her journey!

Petition One: To Christ But Not Rightly

To understand this first petition or request made of Jesus, we must note that the Mark account records that this Gentile woman had heard of Jesus and most likely knew of His miracles from at least one other source. However she heard, she found hope, and that hope was to jump-start her faith in and relationship with Jesus.

Her petition for help was made directly to Jesus, "Have mercy on me, Lord, Son of David." The petition was directed to the right person (Jesus) with humility (as she fell at His feet), but she based her request on Him being the Son of David. She was not Jewish, and hence she had no right or inheritance to ground her request on Jesus being the Son of David. The Scriptures record that she kept making the same petition. She persisted in her repetition of that request, yet the response of Jesus was silence for "He did not answer her a word."

The silence of heaven to one's prayer can be one of the most exasperating experiences of life because we don't understand the silence. If we were obedient to the psalmist's words, "Cease striving (or be still) and know that I am God" (Psalm 46:10), we would be familiar with the essence of silence before God. There are three possible responses to God's silence. First, we just keep asking the same thing time after time. Maybe God didn't hear me or maybe He is waiting for me to repeat the request a certain number of times so that He knows that I'm serious. This seems to have been the reasoning behind the Gentile woman's repeated petition directed solely at Jesus. A second response to such silence might lead the petitioner to reexamine his or her own heart for sin or for not asking in the right way or not basing the request on the right promise. And a third response to such deafening silence is that maybe one needs to enlist others to help in asking God for help. That's what happens in the second petition!

Petition Two: To Christ but through Friends

The direct and persistent appeal to Jesus for assistance yielded no results outwardly for the Gentile woman. The silence of God, however, is not without purpose! If we respond correctly, it can be one of those tools that the Lord uses to bring us into a deeper relationship with Him. If we don't respond the way God desires, His silence can drive us even farther away from Him. Let's look at this Gentile woman's second petition from Matthew 15:23–24, "And His disciples came and implored [kept asking] Him, saying, 'Send her away, because she keeps shouting at us.' But He answered and said, 'I was sent only to the lost sheep of the house of Israel.' "

When her request met with silence from Jesus, the Gentile woman directed her appeal to Jesus' friends. Seemingly, there has been no change in the grounds or foundation of the prayer (that Jesus was the Son of David). Jesus' disciples had sway with Him, she thought, so whom you know should affect heaven's response. Evidently, she kept asking the disciples and they kept asking Jesus to "send her away." The Gentile woman's persistence is almost like nagging, but the disciples showed no compassion for her and her situation. This petition was not met with silence but with a restriction that Jesus was "sent only to the lost sheep of the house of Israel." This confining restriction could have shut the door completely for the Gentile woman.

Petition Three: To Christ Simply and Humbly

In spite of God's silence, the rejection from the disciples and the restrictions from Jesus Himself, the Gentile woman came once again (synthesis):

> [1]But she came and began to bow down before Him, saying, "Lord, help me!" And He answered and said, [2]"Let the children be satisfied first, for it is not good to take the children's bread and throw it to the dogs" (Matthew 15:25–26; Mark 7:27).

Her petition, "Lord, help me," was very simple, just like Peter's request as he was sinking in the water ("Lord, save me"). But this petition was also wrapped in humility as she bowed down before Him to make it. More important, this woman's request was not based on Jewish grounds but on the fact that Jesus Christ is Lord of all (Acts 10:38). We all make petitions to the Father that are not based on the right aspect of God's Word or His character. Some of us never realize that our petition is wrongly based. We then rationalize away the nonresponse to the petition by saying that it was not God's will. The end result is that we have not grown closer to our Savior and our faith has not increased.

The person trying to walk by faith realizes that "without faith it is impossible to please Him, for he who comes to God must believe that He is and that He is a rewarder of those who seek Him" (Hebrews 11:6). Admirably, this Gentile woman kept seeking the Savior and Lord, no matter what barriers stood in her way. She progresses toward knowing Him better and gaining the request, and her progress in faith was exhibited in her prayer life.

This third petition finally brings an answer directly from Jesus. It is probably not the answer she wanted, but in that answer there was a solution for her need if she would seize upon it. "Let the children be satisfied first." She was a seeker of God, and there was a reward for her in Jesus' words. This Gentile had to grasp His words for herself for the truths to be realized personally.

Petition Four: To Christ with Great Faith

Jesus' answer to her request before had not silenced her, and this answer from Jesus' lips opened up an opportunity:

> [2]But she answered and said to Him, "Yes, Lord, but even the dogs under the table feed on the children's crumbs [1]which fall from their master's table." Then Jesus said to her, "O woman, your faith is great. [2]Because of this answer, [1]it shall be done for you as you wish. [2]Go; the demon has gone out of your daughter." [1]And her daughter was healed at once. [2]And going back to her home, she found the child lying on the bed, the demon having left. (Matthew 15:26–28; Mark 7:28–30)

Her response was one of greater humility as she identified with the dogs under the Master's table. She seized on the importance of the word "first," meaning that there would be an opportunity for the

Gentiles after the gospel was preached to the Jews. She realized that if the gospel and the riches thereof were to come to the Gentiles, why not an exception now? She applied what she knew of Jesus' words to her situation.

Jesus commends the woman's great faith. It was a faith that could take silence, that could grow from the wrong promises to the right promises, that could fight through the barriers that people erected and that could take a hard answer. It was a faith that persevered in light of imperfect knowledge and that could grasp the importance of one word in Jesus' response and apply it directly to her circumstances. It was a faith that was praised, rewarded and grounded in the truth of Jesus' words.

Life Response to Biblical Truth

1. This Canaanite woman, the lowliest of the lowly—who had no grounds for asking, no promises to stand on and very little knowledge of the Lord other than secondhand knowledge—persevered in prayer. "At all times they ought to pray and not to lose heart" (Luke 18:1). Should not we who have grounds to ask the Father, who have a proper position in Christ, who possess greater privileges and promises in Christ and who have a greater true knowledge of Him, persevere even more in prayer?

2. All saints will experience the silence of God to their requests at some time. Of course, "If I

regard wickedness in my heart, the Lord will not hear" (Psalm 66:18). Beyond this, however, God always answers the prayer of the believer. The answer may be direct, delayed or different from what was prayed. The answer may even be that the request is denied.

The delay in answering our prayer, surrounded by the silence of God, may be to test or build our faith, as it was for the Canaanite woman. The delay may be because the spiritual battle is great (Daniel 10:12–13). The delay and silence of God may be a result of the divine order of events taking time to get in place. The delay may provide instructional value by giving us time to reflect on God's words and ways so that we will learn a special lesson (Joshua 7:6–9; Psalm 77:10–12) or perhaps the essence of our original request needs to change. The delay may come as a result of us needing to take action first (Exodus 14:15) or of God having something better for us. It is true that if our request is not in accordance with God's will or glory, it will be flatly denied or reshaped by the hand of God to please Him (John 14:13–14; 1 John 3:21–22).

For this Gentile woman, the delay was a trial, but ultimately it brought out the best in her. While going through the experience was no doubt anguishing, its end result was rewarding because her faith grew and was rewarded. When delay, difference or denial to a request occurs, do we evaluate our original request before the Father? For instance, has God already spoken, but because of our baggage, our activities or our preconceived perspectives we missed it? If so, then we must confess and be still and get to know God (1 John 1:9; Psalm 46:10). Second, maybe our original request reflected our own ambitions, desires and satisfaction. If that is the case, we need to repent and pray according to the will of God. Third, if the silence is a test of our faith, we need to persist and stand on the promises of God, all along seeking to know Him better and better. This woman's response to delays and denial in prayer is an excellent model for us to embrace if we want our faith to grow and become greater.

3. When confronted with silence and denial, the Syrophoenician woman sought others to influence the Son of God by interceding for her. It is scriptural to "bear one another's burdens, and thereby fulfill the law of Christ" (Galatians 6:2), but she did not get a positive response. There was no compassion evidenced by the selfish disciples. It was inconvenient and inappropriate for them to intercede for her. They would much rather send her away. At least the disciples were not hypocrites, saying they would intercede for her and then do nothing. For that, they must be com-

mended! There is nothing wrong with asking others to pray for us, but one must understand that there is no "magic formula" in many praying. The key is one or more praying according to the will of God with the petition nestled in the words of Scripture. If someone asks you to pray for him or her, do not say "yes" unless you actually will. To say "yes" and not pray is destructive to you and your faith as well as the faith and prayer life of the one who seeks your prayers.

4. The request, "Lord, help me," reflects helplessness. Only the helpless can truly pray! Helplessness is the essence of prayer because it recognizes our inability to do anything (humility) and God's capability of doing everything (faith). Ole Hallesby once said, "Helplessness united with faith produces prayer. Without faith our helplessness would only be a vain cry of distress in the night."[2] Pride and strength of the flesh undermine any response of faith.

5. The Gentile woman's third request was preceded by worship, but worship as a once-a-week experience does not make our prayers more effective. According to James 1:26–27, pure and undefiled religion in the sight of our God and Father is having speech that is pure and providing grace for the need of the moment. It is giving service to others in distress and being separated from the world and unto God. This

kind of religion is worship that is a life of obedience. If our life is one of continual worship, then His will should be our will and His desires our prayers. "If you abide in Me, and My words abide in you, ask whatever you wish, and it will be done for you" (John 15:7). Such obedience in the power of the Holy Spirit leads to a richer life of faith. It is a faith that does not stagnate but grows, seizing on the truths and promises of Scripture.

6. This Canaanite woman persisted in her request through the silence, the refusal and the seeming contempt. She clung tenaciously to "one word" of Christ's words for her request. With the one word of hope from the lips of the Living Word, she persisted. Her faith waxed stronger as she reasoned with the words of our Lord. She prayed more and trusted more because of that previous word "first." She quoted back to the Lord His words with a proper understanding of the intent. No wonder our Lord commended her for great faith! She knew that her request, her being, her life and her future depended upon the Word of God. Do we believe likewise?

7. This woman did not trust in methods, proven or unproven. She did not trust in feelings of the Lord's presence or absence of those feelings. Her trust was totally in His person and His word, and so should our trust be. Methods change,

and the effectiveness of methods change. Feelings change; but the Word of God, living and written, does not change and will abide forever (1 Peter 1:23–25).

8. This pilgrimage or progress in prayer resulted in greater communication with our Lord, greater knowledge of Him, greater intimacy with Him, a greater dependence on His Word and greater faith. That should be the desire of all believers! Is it yours?

Questions for Reflection

1. If you sense prayerlessness in your life, have you rationalized it away as a weakness or seen it as sin? Our perspective on prayerlessness will affect our progress or digression in the walk of faith. What is the difference between seeing prayerlessness as weakness or seeing it as sin? Why is the right perspective critical to walking by faith?

2. What is your response to prayers that are answered directly as prayed? That are answered differently than prayed? That are delayed in being answered? That are denied? What commonality should there be in all such responses from the supplicant?

3. As you reflect on the times when God was purposely silent about your petitions, how did these impact your faith in God and His Word?

4. If you have ever persevered in prayer for someone or about something, what did you learn about God and what happened to your faith in Him and His Word?

5. Too busy, too tired, too much to do, too many dis-
    tractions or whatever excuse all undermine our
    prayer life and our faith. How does one proceed to
    disarm the excuses and reclaim the time with God
    in prayer?

6. This Gentile woman's faith was great, but it was not
    an instant deal. Her pilgrimage in prayer and her
    clinging to the spoken Word of God yielded a great
    faith. Can you remember such experiences in your
    life? Express out loud to God and to others what you
    learned and have embraced from these experiences.

7. There is nothing like the pains and problems with
    children that cause God's people to pray more fer-
    vently and more humbly. What pains and problems
    has God used to perfect your prayer life and your
    faith? How have these instances been different in ac-
    complishing what God desired for your life?

Chapter 7

Faith and Stages

Read Matthew 15:29–16:12 and Mark 8:11–26

A life of faith does not consist of a series of random isolated events, where we have an opportunity to respond in faith or not. It is instead a divine process, where events are not random but sovereignly ordained and timed in such a way that if (and that is a big "if" for most of us) we respond correctly, our faith grows and blossoms. From a statistician's perspective, there is a correlation among the type of events, the spacing of the events and the frequency of events as to what God wants to accomplish at a particular time in a believer's life. These events, their spacing and their frequency are hidden from the carnal (fleshly) mind. The believer, who spiritually appraises all things with the mind of Christ, may have an inkling of their purpose initially or may have a retrospective understanding of the events with time. Many may, by faith, grasp the sovereignty of God with these events without understanding the events themselves. In such a case, these events are not faith-crippling with bitterness, disappointment and despair; but the believer moves on knowing that God ultimately will use it all for good in the believer's life and in the lives of others.

On the other hand, failure to respond by faith to these "nonrandom" events does not mean that God gives up on us. He understands our frailty and has contingency plans (although not really contingency plans because of what He has seen and knows when time began—He is never surprised). A nonfaith response to random, isolated, difficult and not-so-difficult events could be very detrimental to our spiritual well-being; but from Matthew chapters 15 and 16 and from the parallel account in Mark 8 we will see how God works to help our faith grow in stages.

Faith and Repeated Experiences

An important part of the context to understanding the events in Matthew 16 and Mark 8 is to grasp the significance of the repeated experiences. What is a repeated experience? A repeated experience is a situation where the divine truths to be learned and applied are the same, but the outward trappings of the circumstance may be similar or diversely different. The previous experiences with bread in the feeding of the five thousand (John 6; Matthew 14; Mark 6; and Luke 9) and the four thousand (Matthew 15:29–39; Mark 8:1–10) are repeats for the disciples. When we blow a divine test or situation, God in His faithfulness, His love and His desire for us to press on to maturity in Christ will bring us back to the experience (usually with subtle differences) to see if we have progressed in faith. The time frame (days, months or years) is unknown, but for sure it will be when least expected. The disciples are returned to a situation where calculation is of no avail, where human alternatives are nonexistent, where compromises produce nothing, where current resources are inadequate and where Christ alone is the source of sufficiency.

To understand repeat events, the two previous repeat experiences are contrasted in Table 7.1 with the feeding of the five thousand and the feeding of the four thousand. Out of the fifteen contrasts, the only true similarity is the sluggishness of the disciples. In Mark 6:52 after the feeding of the five thousand, the Bible says, "They had not gained any insight from the incident of the loaves, but their heart was hardened." The sluggishness of the disciples during the feeding of the four thousand is more explicit as recorded by their words in Mark 8:4, "Where will anyone be able to find enough bread here in this desolate place to satisfy these people?" They had not made the transfer of faith and understanding to the second repeat experience. In one case, Christ was sufficient in the suburbs, and in the other He was sufficient in the wilderness. Christ's sufficiency is not limited by our physical, emotional or mental place.

Table 7.1 Contrast of Two Repeated Experiences: Feeding of the 5000 and the 4000

Contrast	Feeding of the 5000	Feeding of the 4000
1	in all four Gospels	in Matthew/Mark
2	Bethsaida	Decapolis
3	close to city	desolate
4	green grass	ground, desert place
5	Jews mostly	Gentiles mostly
6	at least nine miracles in Capernaum area	at least one miracle (Mark 5:19–20) in the Gerasene region
7	compassion upon sheep without a shepherd	compassion because of hunger
8	one day or less	three days
9	five loaves and two fish	seven loaves and few small fish
10	leftovers – twelve baskets (small)	leftovers – seven baskets (large)
11	Jesus dismissed disciples and people and went to pray	Jesus went with disciples in a boat
12	boat without Jesus, contrary winds and off course	no incident
13	sluggish disciples	sluggish disciples
14	public sermon on Bread of Life	private discourse on bread
15	many disciples withdrew	disciples rebuked, encouraged and taught

Some may say that looking back on such repeated experiences is too retrospective or that hindsight is better than the reality when you are going through it. However, in the Sermon on the Mount, Jesus exhorted the disciples to consider the lilies (to observe thoroughly or to consider accurately and diligently in Matthew 6:28) and to consider the ravens (to perceive clearly in Luke 12:24, 27). This exhortation implies contemplation, effort and correlation of events to make sense of what God may be doing in the world around us. It is true that we are frequently moving through life at such a fast pace that we do not have time to contemplate, meditate or pray about understanding things that God is doing. We all sense demands on our time and energies; but there must be windows of time where we can be still before the Lord and remember His faithfulness, His ways in our past and present, our successes with Him and our failures without Him. Reflecting on such repeat experiences and about His presence (when done in the power of the Holy Spirit) should produce a sense of awe in us and a desire to press on to know Him even better.

Faith Not by Signs

When we miss God's perspectives or lessons in faith through repeated experiences, God, in His graciousness, tries to educate or instruct us in small steps so that we might be more teachable and receptive to the faith response the next time. Sometimes,

this means that He must deal with our religious up-
bringings, our denominational weaknesses and our
corporate mentalities that are far from the mind of
Christ. The event recorded in the Gospels of Matthew (16:1–4) and Mark (8:11–13) could be pieced
together as follows as the first step in instructing
the disciples about what faith is not:

> ¹The Pharisees and Sadducees came up ²and began to
> argue with Him, seeking from Him a sign from heaven,
> to test Him. ¹But He replied to them, "When it is evening,
> you say, 'It will be fair weather, for the sky is red. And
> in the morning, there will be a storm today, for the sky
> is red and threatening.' Do you know how, to discern
> the appearance of the sky, but cannot discern the signs
> of the times?" ²Sighing deeply in His spirit, He said,
> "Why does this generation seek for a sign? ¹An evil and
> adulterous generation seeks after a sign. ²Truly I say to
> you, no sign will be given to this generation, ¹except the
> sign of Jonah." ²Leaving them, He again embarked and
> went away to the other side.

By this time of our Lord's ministry, twenty-three
of the thirty-five recorded miracles in the Gospels
had occurred. In addition, on three prior occasions,
Jews had asked for a sign (John 2:18; Matthew 12:38;
John 6:30). It is no wonder that Jesus groaned deeply
in His spirit at the unbelief of the Pharisees and Sadducees, in light of the tremendous evidence of who
He was. "Jews ask for signs and Greeks search for
wisdom" (1 Corinthians 1:22), but true believers are
to "walk by faith, not by sight" (2 Corinthians 5:7).

The discussion that Jesus had with the Pharisees and Sadducees was also for the benefit of the Jewish disciples who had to unlearn that faith is not by signs. Their Jewish and religious upbringing, legalism and teaching of the Word devoid of the Spirit would have corrupted their proper understanding of walking by faith without signs. Walking by sight or signs never leads to solid, definable faith; it only leads to wanting more signs. Gideon in Judges chapters 6 through 8 is an excellent example of someone who walked by signs. His faith had momentary blossoms but never reached the richness that God desired. In John 6:2, 14–15, 26, the progression of those who seek signs is exposed. Throwing aside concern for God's will and timing, people driven by signs will tend to use force to accomplish their purposes or to maintain their prosperity. Is it possible that the use of business methodologies and strategies in churches today is a coercive effort to maintain purposes and prosperity that leave God out of the equation? The foundations of what Jesus Christ wanted to accomplish in His disciples as to walking by faith could only be realized if He repeatedly dealt with the misconceptions, distortions and blasphemies that they had been raised with in the religious establishment of their time.

Faith That Is Weak Is Queried

The second step in the disciples' reeducation process involved a question-and-answer interchange between the Lord and them. When we do not understand or grasp a truth, God sometimes communicates to us what is not the case before there is a restatement of the truth of what the reality is.

> [2]And they had forgotten to take bread, and did not have more than one loaf in the boat with them. [1]And the disciples came to the other side of the sea. [2]And He was giving orders to them, saying, "Watch out and beware of [1]the leaven of the Pharisees and Sadducees and [2]of Herod." They began to discuss with one another the fact that they had no bread. [1]But Jesus, aware of this, said, "You men of little faith, why do you discuss among yourselves that you have no bread? [2]Do you not yet see or understand? Do you have a hardened heart? Having eyes do you not see? And having ears, do you not hear? And do you not remember, when I broke the five loaves for the five thousand, how many baskets full of broken pieces you picked up?" They said to Him, "Twelve." "When I broke the seven for the four thousand, how many large baskets full of broken pieces did you pick up?" And they said to Him, "Seven." And He was saying to them, "Do you not yet understand [1]that I did not speak to you concerning bread? But beware of the leaven of the Pharisees and the Sadducees." Then they understood that He did not say to beware of the leaven of bread, but of the teaching of the Pharisees and Sadducees. (Matthew 16:5–12; Mark 8:14–21)

This interchange between the Lord and the disciples was brought about by the fact that they had no more than one loaf of bread with them and that the Lord said to "beware of the leaven of the Pharisees, of the Sadducees and of Herod." Initially, the disciples took Jesus' comment literally, but later they understood that Jesus was referring to the teachings of these groups. The Pharisees were the religious experts of their day; and they were consumed with formalism, traditions of men, legalism, hypocrisy and hunger for power and control over others. The Sadducees were the philosophers of the time. They believed that since there would be no resurrection and no immortality, one must live for the moment now. The Herodians were the politicians, the extreme secularists of the culture, who wielded power and force to do their own thing or to accomplish their own desires now. The leaven that Jesus warned the disciples of was the contaminating influence from each that starts at different places but always ends up focusing on the temporal things of life, such as wealth, power, control and irrelevant stuff. The end result of this influence is blindness and unbelief, a position that Jesus sensed in the disciples as reflected by His statement in Matthew 16:8, "You men of little faith."

Since the disciples were in a quagmire of unbelief, even with the recent repeated experiences of bread at the feeding of the five thousand and the four thousand, Jesus knew that there had to be some probing of the disciples' current spiritual state. His eight questions came in three clusters. The first cluster of five questions from Jesus follows:

1. [1]You men of little faith, why do you discuss among yourselves that you have no bread?

2. [2]Do you not yet see or understand?

3. [2]Do you have a hardened heart?

4. [2]Having eyes, do you not see?

5. [2]And having ears, do you not hear?

In this barrage of questions from Jesus, there was no verbal response from the disciples, most likely because of the convicting nature of the queries. The disciples were worried about bread (temporal), yet the Bread of Life was with them. Their lack of understanding revealed hardened hearts, something no disciple of Jesus wants to admit openly. Their senses were dulled by unbelief. Jesus had accurately pegged them as men of little faith, but that is not where they should have been.

The second cluster of questions is unique in that Jesus does get a response from the disciples, but the response is one of physical fact and not of spiritual significance:

6. [2]"Do you not remember when I broke the five loaves for the five thousand, how many baskets full of broken pieces did you pick up?" They said to Him, "Twelve."

7. [2]"When I broke the seven for the four thousand, how many large baskets full of broken pieces did you pick up?" And they said to Him, "Seven."

Since Jesus received no answers from the five convicting questions, He asked two simple questions that only required remembering the details of the leftovers. The disciples had been responsible for distributing the bread and fish as well as collecting the leftovers in baskets. They knew what He had started with and what He had ended up with. The remembrance of these details should have jump-started their thinking or helped them to connect the dots, leading to faith in Him. However, the third query "cluster" contained only one question:

8. "Do you not yet understand?"

This question was answered by their silence because they did not understand. Their faith was weak!

Faith Is in Stages

The essence of the eight questions from Jesus was to awaken the disciples' faith and move them out of their stagnancy and sluggishness of heart. By the end of these accounts in Matthew 16 and Mark 8, one might think that Jesus had failed or given up. However, the ultimate Teacher knows that sometimes one needs to communicate truth in a variety of ways before a person grasps it. An object lesson given in Mark's Gospel shows that the Lord had not given up.

And they came to Bethsaida. And they brought a blind man to Jesus and implored Him to touch him. Taking the blind man by the hand, He brought him out of the village; and after spitting on his eyes and laying His hands on him, He asked him, "Do you see anything?" And he looked up and said, "I see men, for I see them like trees, walking around." Then again He laid His hands on his eyes; and he looked intently and was restored, and began to see everything clearly. And He sent him to his home, saying, "Do not even enter the village." (Mark 8:22–26)

Of the thirty-five specific miracles recorded in the Gospels, five deal with blindness. This particular miracle is the third one relating to blindness, probably occurring, as did the remaining two, during Jesus' last year of ministry. What is unique about this miracle compared to all of the rest of the miracles is that it took two tries to heal the man. Jesus' power was not insufficient to heal the man in one try, but the two tries were sovereignly intended to educate the disciples that faith progresses in stages.

Table 7.2 is a contrast of what transpires in this miracle and what had and would occur for the disciples. This blind man was healed in two stages, and it would take stages for the disciples to see clearly as well. They were seeing vaguely and only parts, but the day would come that they would see and see perfectly.

Table 7.2 Contrast of the Blind Man and the Disciples

Blind man	Blind disciples
Led by the hand of Jesus	Led by Jesus
Removed from city of unbelief	Removed from culture of unbelief
Spit from His mouth	Words from His mouth
Touch of His hands	Works of His hands
Query: Do you see anything?	Query: Do you not yet understand?
First touch: seeing vaguely	First touch: disciples understanding only parts
Second touch: seeing perfectly	Second touch: when Holy Spirit given
Sent home	Sent to the world
Told not to enter village of unbelief	Told to shake off the dust of your feet in such places

The idea of stages in the life of faith is communicated in several other places in the New Testament, such as Mark 4:26–28. In this passage, Jesus says,

> The kingdom of God is like a man who casts seed upon the soil; and he goes to bed at night and gets up by day, and the seed sprouts and grows—how, he himself does not know. The soil produces crops by itself; first the blade, then the head, then the mature grain in the head.

There are three stages of growth hinted at here as well as in 1 John 2:13, where three stages of faith or maturity are referenced (fathers, young men and children): "I am writing to you, fathers, because you know Him who has been from the beginning. I am writing to you, young men, because you have overcome the evil one. I have written to you, children, because you know the Father."

Another critical passage in understanding that faith is by stages is recorded in Luke 8:18: "So take care how you listen; for whoever has, to him more shall be given; and whoever does not have, even what he thinks he has shall be taken away from him." No matter what place or stage we are at in the Christian life, we must pay close attention to God's voice if we want to progress in the life of faith. That implies not only that the heart is humble and receptive to the Word (James 1:21) but also that the Word is heard and obeyed. If the individual is just a hearer of the Word and not a doer, then that which he heard—which he thinks he knows—will be lost. On the other hand, the individual that "looks intently at the perfect law, the law of liberty, and abides by it, not having become a forgetful hearer but an effectual doer, this man will be blessed in what he does" (James 1:25).

The believer hearing and applying that Word to his life will not lose what he has heard. The believer who hears and does not apply the Word to his own personal life, however, will lose the truth and the blessings that accompany this truth. What comes out of repeated experiences and these events of Matthew 16 and Mark 8 is that the Lord is patient with us and He knows that there are certain truths that we will not get without several exposures. The disciples had the Son of God in their presence, and they could not connect the dots in the progression of faith: But when the Holy Spirit comes, He guides them into all truth (John 16:13).

Life Response to Biblical Truth

1. We each need to honestly ask ourselves if we are teachable. Do we learn from past failures and mistakes? Do we find ourselves in repeated experiences? If so, do we get frustrated with God for taking us into these repeated situations? Do we have a lifestyle that allows us to meditate and correlate under the power of the Holy Spirit about God's workings in our life? Do we understand from God's perspective that there are no random, isolated events in life but sovereignly timed events that have divine purpose and from which, if we respond correctly, our faith grows?

   God loves us so much that He will faithfully return us, time after time, to our private or public, secret or known failures or weaknesses. We will be brought to a desolate/desert place (whether it be physically, emotionally or mentally), reeducated as to what our response should be and stripped of all options except one: Jesus Christ. The timing, duration and unique placement of this experience will be sovereignly arranged by

God. If we respond by faith, we will come to new realizations about His sufficiency as the Bread of Life. A continual nonfaith response to random and nonrandom, unique and not-so-unique and difficult and not-so-difficult events could be very detrimental to our spiritual well-being. Bitterness toward God, others or life in general could set in and destroy us and others (Hebrews 12:15).

2. Repeated experiences are part of the divine process. As believers, we will all pass through them. These divinely ordained experiences are not the same for every believer. They will come uniquely cloaked in such a way they do not look the same outwardly, but the inward work they are to accomplish is the same. The disciples were sluggish or had hardened hearts, and they did not see the spiritual realities Jesus wanted them to see. We need to be honest with ourselves before God that we are no different than the disciples. We will have our times of sluggishness and hardness of heart. Whether this sluggishness is for hours or days, weeks or months or years or decades makes a difference in the divine scheme. Sad to say, many believers have been sluggish in the life of faith for a very long time. The author of Hebrews 5:12 says, "For though by this time you ought to be teach-ers, you have need again for someone to teach you the elementary principles of the oracles of

God, and you have come to need milk and not solid food." Thus, one surefire indicator of this sluggishness in faith is the continual consumption of the more elementary principles from the Word of God. A second indicator is the lack of time for meditation on, reflection on and correlation of what God is doing in our lives under the power of the Holy Spirit.

3. "We walk by faith, not by sight" (2 Corinthians 5:7). We do not walk by "fleeces" or signs, by repeated successes, by successful methods elsewhere or by what just feels right. The seeking of signs is not a norm for living by faith but an extreme exception. The young and the weak in faith look for signs (see Gideon in Judges chapters 6 through 8), but those who want to mature in the faith must lay aside these efforts.

4. The disciples had misconceptions and distortions from their religious upbringing, their culture, their professions and their associations that contaminated the truths of walking by faith. Still, Jesus gently used the Word to correct those errors. Biblical thinking, spiritual vision and faith living are undermined by the false teaching of spiritual things from the religious experts, rational things from the philosophers and political things from the politicians of our day. We still need to be aware of false doctrine from the spiritual, from the rational and from

the political minds of today. Our minds must be renewed daily from the Word of God as we depend upon the Holy Sprit to teach us.

5. After some repeated experiences and after some discussion about what faith is not, Jesus queried the disciples' weak faith with three clusters of questions. The first cluster of questions was convicting queries that pointed out that they had not learned from repeated experiences. The second cluster of questions required some reflection and remembrance of past events while the third and final cluster noted that even with His help they still did not understand. Do we have relationships with other believers that are deep and that would allow such convicting interactions? These kinds of interchanges can only happen in a discipling relationship with two or more believers. We all need accountability for our faith to grow and blossom, and that interchange cannot happen in a large group or a multitude of disciples!

6. Even though we may have been in the spiritual in-crowd for many years, had excellent teaching, been exposed to much truth and even seen miracles galore, we may be in stage one of discipleship (just as the twelve disciples were) because of the littleness or staleness of our faith. We could be in this stage for years or even our whole life. As noted earlier, we need account-

ability to others who will say the hard things we do not want to hear or ask the hard questions we do not want to answer. Being discipled and discipling others is critical for our faith to have an environment to blossom!

7. It is very evident from this study that there are stages in the life of faith. Even so, may we be less concerned about the stage we are in and more concerned about our solitary focus on Jesus Christ. Can we pray as follows?

    Jesus, grasp my hand, and lead me out of the unbelief lifestyle and mind-set. Touch my eyes and heart with Your words and help me to recognize Your works. I want to see clearly, not only partially. If I have not been teachable, remind me and teach me again. I want Your will, Your best for my life.

8. Faith is not faith in faith! As Tozer once said, "Faith in faith is faith astray."[1] Our faith needs to be rightly placed before it is right! We must have faith or trust in God's Word and in the person of God Himself as we obey that written Word and the living Word.

Questions for Reflection

1. Have you experienced some repeated experiences or trials over the past year or years where God was trying to get your attention and help you ingrain some biblical truth into your life? What was the commonality of such situations for you and what do you think God was trying to communicate? If you keep a journal, these kinds of questions might be easier to answer. Otherwise, you will need an extended time alone with God for honest answers.

2. It is critical to understand that all believers get caught in a quagmire of unbelief for various lengths of time. What did you learn about yourself and about God from those situations? How did God extract you from the quagmire?

3. These repeated experiences are nonrandom events sovereignly arranged by God to renew, redirect or mature our faith. What was your response while going through them? What would your response be now in light of God's Word?

4. Signs that our faith is very weak include: no insight from our experiences, sluggishness in understanding, blindness, hard of hearing, continually needing milk and not solid food, seeking signs and more. Do you have or are you cultivating deep biblical relationships with other believers who could ask you convicting questions about your faith or relationship with the Lord? What questions would they ask you? What kind of environment is critical for this to happen?

5. Can you identify the stage of faith you are in? Child, young man or father? Or child, young woman or older woman (Titus 2)? Why do you think that you are in that stage? What would your close biblical friends say?

6. As we have seen God's patience in dealing with the disciples and trying to mold their faith in Him, how has your perspective of God, His character and His ways been enlarged?

7. To be able to transfer walking by faith from one situation to another is essential to the quality of our faith. What have you learned about yourself and about God when you have correctly made the transfer of faith and when you have failed?

Chapter 8

Faith and Failure

Read Matthew 17:1–21; Mark 9:1–29; Luke 9:28–43

Somehow there has been a serious perverted exchange of faith and success in our day in that the two are equated in many Christian circles. If one is successful, he or she has done it by faith in God. If an individual is not successful, then he or she is not walking by faith. Some would say that this perversion is the result of the health, wealth and prosperity gospel while others might argue that it is another illustration of the large corporate business model undermining and replacing the biblical model. I expect that influences from both mind-sets are part of the problem.

A passage from Numbers 20:1–13 provides a backdrop for this faith and success dilemma. The sons of Israel were on the verge of entering the Promised Land, but there was no water. The second generation of Israelites complained and grumbled at Moses and Aaron just as their parents had done almost forty years prior. God told Moses to take his rod, to assemble the congregation and to speak to the rock before their eyes. Moses obeyed two-thirds of what God said, but he became very impatient as he projected the consistent complaining pattern of the parents onto their children. Instead of speaking to the rock, he struck the rock. Of course, the Rock, Christ, was to be struck only once and not twice (this was the second instance)—this is important imagery. However, water came forth abundantly from the rock even in Moses' disobedience. Why did not God just hold back the water? The answer seems to be that the need of the people was great so God met that need and dealt with Moses privately for not treating Him as holy in the sight of the people. The point to be made is that even though there was a tremendous, visible success regarding water, it was not done by faith. Outward visible success and faith are not necessarily correlated in the spiritual realm!

In a piece entitled "Faith Dares to Fail," Tozer also addresses this perversion of faith and success. A long quote drives home the point:

> Our Lord died an apparent failure, discredited by the leaders of established religion, rejected by society and

forsaken by His friends. The man who ordered Him to the cross was the successful statesman whose hand the ambitious hack politician kissed. It took the resurrection to demonstrate how gloriously Christ had triumphed and how tragically the governor had failed. . . . God may allow His servant to succeed when He has disciplined him to a point where he does not need to succeed to be happy. The man who is elated by success and cast down by failure is still a carnal man. At best his fruit will have a worm in it. God will allow His servant to succeed when he has learned that success does not make him dearer to God nor more valuable in the total scheme of things. We cannot buy God's favor with crowds or converts or new missionaries sent out or Bibles distributed. All these things can be accomplished without the help of the Holy Spirit. . . . We can afford to follow Him to failure. Faith dares to fail. The resurrection and the judgment will demonstrate before all worlds who won and who lost.[1]

As one examines the Scriptures, one can see that others besides Jesus, such as Noah, Jeremiah and John the Baptist, had a lot of outward failure but exhibited much faith. This intertwining of faith and failure brings us to parallel accounts in Matthew 17, Mark 9 and Luke 9. In these biblical accounts, we shall see that failure is not independent of place or situation, it is not independent of the best people or the second string and it is not unrelated to timing whether or not it is an opportune or inopportune time. It is something that all of us who want to know the living God better will experience, for without such experiences we may have warped conceptions of God, His ways and His purposes. The psalmist rightly says, "For all things are Your servants" (Psalm 119:91), and failure is one of those God things that serves God well.

Deep Truths

The events of Matthew 17, Mark 9 and Luke 9 are sandwiched between two critical revelations that occurred days before and a few days afterward. Matthew 16:21–23 and Mark 8:31–35 provide tremendous insight into the events to come:

> From that time Jesus began to show His disciples that He must go to Jerusalem, and suffer many things from the elders and chief priests and scribes, and be killed, and be raised up on the third day. Peter took Him aside and began to rebuke Him, saying, "God forbid it, Lord! This shall never happen to You." But He turned and said to Peter, "Get behind Me, Satan! You are a stumbling block to Me; for you are not setting your mind on God's interests, but man's." (Matthew 16:21–23)

> And He began to teach them that the Son of Man must suffer many things and be rejected by the elders and the chief priests and the scribes, and be killed, and after three days rise again. And He was stating the matter plainly. And Peter took Him aside and began to rebuke Him. But turning around and seeing His disciples, He rebuked Peter and said, "Get behind Me, Satan; for you are not setting your mind on God's interests, but man's." And He summoned the crowd with His disciples, and said to them, "If anyone wishes to come after Me, he must deny himself, and take up his cross and follow Me. For

whoever wishes to save his life will lose it, but whoever loses his life for My sake and the gospel's will save it." (Mark 8:31–35)

From the chronological structure of the gospel of Mark, we know that this is the first time that Jesus talked of His suffering, rejection, death and resurrection. The Mark account tells us that He stated the matter plainly to the disciples this first time. The second account of such conversations comes after the failure on the mountaintop and in the valley of real life. Mark 9:30–32 is a record of this second interaction:

From there they went out and began to go through Galilee, and He did not want anyone to know about it. For He was teaching His disciples and telling them, "The Son of Man is to be delivered into the hands of men, and they will kill Him; and when He has been killed, He will rise three days later." But they did not understand this statement, and they were afraid to ask Him.

Jesus was still teaching the disciples about His death and His resurrection, but they did not understand yet, even with this second repetition of truth. Not only did they not understand, but also they were afraid to ask questions about the teaching. The third repetition of these truths on His suffering, death and resurrection occurs in Mark 10:32–34, where more details on the suffering are included as Jesus approaches Jerusalem for the final days. The first and second conversations about these deep truths are the pieces of bread that sandwich the events that God will use to break down the disciples' hardness of heart and sluggishness of mind.

The essence of this interchange between Jesus and His disciples was to communicate what was to happen in the future with His suffering, death and resurrection. These were deep truths that the disciples did not understand or even question. Likewise, the Apostle Paul, in the 6th chapter of Romans, talks of our identification with Christ, our crucifixion in Christ, our death in Christ and our resurrection in Christ. Again, these are deep truths, which most believers do not understand or ask about even today. The additional sadness surrounding these deep truths today is that they are seldom taught in a simple and straightforward way. God may have to use suffering and failure in our lives if we are to understand these deep truths so that our faith can blossom.

Dilemma of Faith and Failure

The passage from the Gospel of Luke, "On the next day, when they came down from the mountain, a large crowd met Him" (9:37), is the connection between two places—the mountaintop where Jesus was transfigured before three disciples and the valley where the nine disciples had failed in healing a father's only son. Table 8.1 contrasts the two situations from Matthew 17, Mark 9 and Luke 9.

Table 8.1 Mountaintop and Valley Contrasts

Contrast	Mountaintop	Valley
1	Three disciples	Nine disciples
2	No crowd	Large crowd
3	Jesus	No Jesus
4	To pray	No praying
5	Conversations about departure	Arguments with scribes
6	Disciples sleeping, literally	Disciples asleep in power, i.e., powerless in meeting needs
7	Son of God transfigured	Violent transformation of son
8	Failure	Failure
9	Admonition	Admonition

On the mountaintop, everything seemed perfect: Jesus, peace and quiet, the three disciples (Peter, James and John—the inner circle of men) and time to pray (Luke 9:28). However, some additional insights are given into the events: "And behold, two men were talking with Him; and they were Moses and Elijah, who, appearing in glory, were speaking of His departure which He was about to accomplish at Jerusalem" (Luke 9:30–31). To be sure, this mountaintop experience was to preview His glory and person to His inner circle of men (a divine perspective). However, in light of Jesus' recent teaching on His coming suffering, death and resurrection and the disciples' inability to understand these truths, it seems from the human perspective that Jesus needed encouragement from those who had departed this earth uniquely before. That encouragement or understanding was not coming from this inner core of disciples so God provided another way for it to occur. As with most mountaintop experiences, the three disciples (especially Peter) were enamored with the moment but did not understand its significance. The end result was failure by the three disciples in an ideal environment as exhibited by their sleepiness and sluggishness to understand. The actual admonition on failure for this inner core of men did not come from Jesus' lips, but from the lips of the Father: "This is My Son, My Chosen One; listen to Him!"

They had heard Jesus' words about His coming suffering, death and resurrection; but they had not listened with their heart. What He had said did not translate into their grid of thinking. Tozer communicates this same thought: "God will speak to the hearts of those who prepare themselves to hear; and conversely, those who do not so prepare themselves will hear nothing even though the Word of God is falling upon their outer ears every Sunday."[2]

Ideal environments, perfect teachers, powerful truths and the best of saints do not guarantee that spiritual truths will sink into the heart and bear forth fruit. Even in such ideal situations, failure can occur when least expected. This failure can be a strange minister of God, but it will accomplish

God's purposes in our lives as we come to embrace the deep truths that we have ignored or misunderstood.

In the valley, the situation was surely confusing! The nine disciples were confronted with a need that they had dealt with before on at least two occasions. In Matthew 10:1, the twelve were sent out with authority to cast out unclean spirits, and in Luke 10:1–20 the seventy (of which it is expected that the twelve were a part of this group) were given authority over demons as well. There were at least two previous successes, so this father's demon-possessed son should have been another success. However, God's servants are primed for failure when they try to repeat the successes of the past with the methods or procedures belonging to another time or place. When the focus is not on the Word of God and the Lord God Himself and Him alone, we tend to get in trouble in ministry or in life. The essence of that trouble is not realized immediately but later in time. The finite mind of man seriously struggles in correlating the current difficulty with God's Word or principles in times past. What is necessary to expose this failing is deep times in the Scriptures in the power of the Holy Spirit.

In the valley, the situation was very chaotic—not peace and quiet but more like a three-ring circus. The synthesis of the Matthew, Mark and Luke accounts captures this chaos well:

[2]When they came back to the disciples, they saw a large crowd around them, and some scribes arguing with them. Immediately when the entire crowd saw Him, they were amazed and began running up to greet Him. And He asked them, "What are you discussing with them?"

[3]And a man from the crowd shouted, saying ([2]answered Him) [1]falling on his knees before Him, [3]"Teacher, I beg You to look at my son.

[1]Lord, have mercy on my son [3]for he is my only boy." [2]"Teacher, I brought You my son

[a] [1]for he is an epileptic [NASB, 1963] and is very ill

[b] [2]possessed with a spirit, which makes him mute [[2]also deaf]

[c] [2]and whenever it seizes him, [3](he suddenly screams)

[d] [2]and it slams him to the ground [3](and it throws him into convulsion)

[e] [2]and he foams at the mouth, and grinds his teeth and stiffens out

[f] [3]and only with difficulty does it leave him, mauling him as it leaves.

[g] [1]for he often falls into the fire, and often into the water.

[1]I brought him to Your disciples, and [3]begged Your disciples to cast it out [1]and they could not cure him. And Jesus answered and said, "You unbelieving and perverted generation, how long shall I be with you?

How long shall I put up with you?"
(Matthew 17:14–17; Mark 9:14–19; Luke 9:37–41)

The chaos of the situation is evidenced by the failure of the disciples to deal with the demon in the father's only son; the anguish of the father; the periodic display of thrashing and turmoil by the demon in the son; the crowd expecting a miracle and nothing happening; and the scribes arguing with the disciples as to why neither they nor the name of Jesus could succeed. On top of all of this, the child was very ill as he was an epileptic, demon possessed, deaf and mute, suicidal, mauled by the demon with scarcely any relief and withering away (as noted in the synthesis by the seven levels from [a] to [g]). The illness of the son was a parent's worst nightmare, and it seems that from what Jesus says later the disciples did not understand the depths of the illness.

Jesus arrives into this circus setting, and the crowd leaves the nine disciples and runs to Jesus. The scribes stop arguing, the crowd is watching and the nine disciples appear to be off the hook. The father explains to Jesus the illness of his son, how he specifically brought him to His disciples for help, how he even begged them to cast the demon out and how there was nothing but failure from them. With the response of the father fresh in His ears, Jesus reproves the father who was lacking in faith, the scribes who were antagonistic to the faith and the Messiah and the crowd who may have been looking for signs. Jesus seems grieved with such unbelief in a generation, in a group (the scribes), in an individual (a father) and even in His disciples, who have been affected by the culture of unbelief around them.

Without question the Savior still grieves over unbelief in a generation, a group or an individual today. Can we hear His words of reproof or are our hearts hardened? Or maybe as a society, as groups in that society and as individuals in that society, we have constructed defense mechanisms that protect us from failure and from the truth that "all things are Your servants" (Psalm 119:91).

Dawning of Faith

This scene of failure, anguish, unmet needs, de-moniac conflict and theological discussions seems impossible to resolve. However, it is in these im-possible moments that hope and faith can blossom if we listen closely and grasp the truth revealed to us. The main account for the dawning of faith comes from the Mark account, with snippets from the other two Gospels:

> [2]"Bring him to Me!" They brought the boy to Him. [3]While he was still approaching, [2]he saw Him, immediately the spirit threw him into a convulsion, and falling to the ground, he began rolling around and foaming at the mouth. And He asked his father, "How long has this been happening to him?" And he said, "From childhood. It has often thrown him both into the fire and into the water to destroy him. But if You can do anything, take pity on

us and help us!" And Jesus said to him, 'If you can?' All
things are possible to him who believes." Immediately
the boy's father cried out and said, "I do believe; help
my unbelief." When Jesus saw that a crowd was rapidly
gathering, He rebuked the unclean spirit, saying to it,
"You deaf and mute spirit, I command you, come out of
him and do not enter him again." After crying out and
throwing him into terrible convulsions, it came out; and
the boy became so much like a corpse that most of them
said, "He is dead!" But Jesus took him by the hand and
raised him; and he got up. ¹The boy was cured at once.
³[And He] gave him back to his father. And they were
all amazed at the majesty [NASB, literal translation] of
God. (Matthew 17:17–18; Mark 9:19–27; Luke 9:41–43)

For faith to come to fruition, we must hear as the
Syrophoenician woman heard when she seizes on
the word "first" from Jesus' lips (Mark 7:24–30 and
Matthew 15:21–28). This woman's faith was great;
and if we are honest with ourselves before God,
99.9% of us are not where that woman was. Instead,
we are at the place in life spiritually where this father was, trying to assimilate the truth spoken from
the lips of the Savior.

A single, simple, unrepeated divine command
was spoken, "Bring him to Me!" Whether or not this
father heard the command is difficult to tell from
Scripture. I think he did; but if he did not, he would
have seen the disciples or others taking his son to
Jesus. The words of the Lord Jesus Christ or the actions of those moving the need closer to our Savior
should have been a springboard for the faith of the

father. Anyone familiar with Jesus' ministry would know that the boy being brought to Jesus was not to make him a point of theological discussion but to provide true help. It seems that the father missed the significance of Jesus' words and the movements of his son closer to Jesus Himself, which is the way of most believers today!

Whatever the need or situation, whenever there is movement toward Jesus for the solution, the conflict increases. In this case, the conflict was demoniac as the demon saw Jesus and knew that his time was limited. Seemingly, a bad situation had become worse for a moment. In these situations, we need to cling to the simple divine command of Jesus that we heard spoken specifically to us and our need.

In the midst of this conflict, there is a short delay with Jesus' query to the father, "How long has this been happening to him?" This query seems strange in that Jesus, with His omniscience, surely knew the answer before He asked. If that is true, then this query was not for His own information but rather for His disciples, the father and anyone else close enough to observe or overhear the conversation. With the failure of the nine disciples to cast the demon out, it was important for them to realize that the problem was long-term (from childhood) and extremely intense.

Surely, the father's faith had been undermined by the disciples' failure to cure his only son, just as today's common saints have their faith undermined by the failure of spiritual leadership. Jesus knew where the father was in his faith, but He knew that the father needed to realize where he was himself. With Jesus asking the question of how long, the father is moved toward direct communication with the Savior as he clarified for all listening that the demoniac possession had been from childhood and furthermore that it had been accompanied with suicidal tendencies. The father adds, "But if You can do anything, take pity on us and help us."

Direct, open and honest conversations with the Father will expose the reality of our hearts. It is evident that the faith of the father is deficient! Certainly, there was faith displayed in bringing the son to the nine disciples, but their failure and the wild and confusing atmosphere undermined that faith. Also, the faith of the father was deficient as evidenced by the father not understanding the significance of the command to bring the son to Jesus. In the context of this weak or deficient faith, the father still asks Jesus for compassion and assistance.

Our Lord detected the father's lack of faith in His ability to cure the boy and quickly reprimanded him. It seems that the faith of the father had been undermined by the duration and severity of the son's sickness as well as by the failure and weak faith of the spiritual leaders (the nine disciples) to perform the specific cure. However, the object of faith is not circumstances, not faith itself and not men. It is the Lord Himself. "All things are possible to him who believes" was the refrain from our Lord's lips, reminiscent of the prophet Jeremiah's record from the lips of God, "Behold, I am the LORD, the God of all flesh; is anything too difficult for Me?" (Jeremiah 32:27)

As parents, we secretly hope and pray that we will never go through such agony and pain with a child, especially an only child. However, let us be sure that when everything seems to be crumbling around us, God is in control. He uses the agonies of life, particularly through our children, to draw us to Him. He uses these, most likely, because we would not draw near to Him otherwise due to our fleshly tendency to self-sufficiency. This father recognized that he had faith but not as strong as needed, so he besought Jesus to help his weak or deficient faith become stronger. The father did not look to people or the current religious establishment, but he fixed his eyes on Jesus, the author and perfecter of faith (Hebrews 12:2). He did not fix his eyes on more service, more praying and more knowledge; but he focused on the words of our Lord Jesus, "All things are possible to him who believes." May our focus be likewise that we too may see the dawning and growth of our faith in a great God!

Discussion of Faith and Failure

In light of the failure to cast the demon out of a father's son, it is refreshing that the disciples didn't go and lick their wounds in silence. They truly wanted to understand why they could not cast it out. Was the problem with their faith? Or the circumstances? Matthew 17:19–21 and Mark 9:28–29 record this powerful pedagogical discussion on faith and failure:

> [2]When He came into the house, His disciples began questioning Him privately, "Why could we not drive it out?" [1]And He said to them, "Because of the littleness of your faith; for truly I say to you, if you have faith the size of a mustard seed, you will say to this mountain, 'Move from here to there,' and it will move; and nothing will be impossible to you. [2]"This kind cannot come out by anything but prayer." (Matthew 17:19–21, Mark 9:28–29)

Jesus' answer as to why they could not cast the demon out was that they did not rightly understand their faith or their circumstances. It is interesting to note that this discussion was not public but privately held.

Jesus quickly addresses the first problem with their failure as their "littleness of faith" or their lack of dependence upon God. They could have been trusting in their previous successes, their past experiences, their numbers (there were nine of them and this was only one demon), their allegiance to Christ or even themselves. However, the faith of yesterday or yesteryear is insufficient for the difficulties of today. We cannot ever ride on the laurels of our past faith or on the faith of our parents or mentors and please God in what we are doing. Those situations are important milestones and building blocks to provide impetus to future trust in the Lord and His word, but there are no guarantees that past success in the life of faith automates future success.

Warren Wiersbe notes this about the failure of the nine in the valley:[3]

> The nine were perhaps jealous because they had not been called to go to the mountaintop with Jesus. During the Lord's absence, they began to grow self-indulgent. They neglected prayer; their faith weakened. Then, when the crisis came, they went out to battle without realizing that their power was gone (Judges 16:20). From this example, we see the importance of staying spiritually healthy.

While Wiersbe's observations are very helpful, there may be more to it. It is no coincidence that this is the fifth time that "little faith" or "littleness of faith" has been addressed:

1. "You of little faith" in the Sermon on the Mount (Matthew 6:30);

2. "Why are you afraid, you men of little faith?" or "Where is your faith?" or "Do you still have no faith?" after the storm on the sea (Matthew 8:18–27; Mark 4:35–41; Luke 8:22–25);

3. "You of little faith, why did you doubt?" after Peter sinks in the water (Matthew 14:22–33);

4. "You men of little faith, why do you discuss among yourselves that you have no bread?" (Matthew 16:8) after the feeding of the four thousand (Matthew 15:29–38; Mark 8:1–9) but before healing the blind man in stages (Mark 8:22–26).

5. "Why could we not drive it out?" And He said to
    them, "Because of the littleness of your faith" (Mat-
    thew 17:19–21).

For over two years our Lord had been gently
chiding the disciples for their littleness of faith.
During that same time frame He had pointed out
those with great faith, including the centurion
(Matthew 8:5–13; Luke 7:1–10) and the Syrophoenician woman (Matthew 15:21–28; Mark 7:24–30).
Sad to say, most with great faith at that time were
outside the established religious norms. The failure
of the inner core of disciples on the mountaintop, as
well as the nine in the valley along with the previous experiences of little faith over the past two plus
years, shows that this malady of little faith affected
all of the disciples. Indeed, none had grasped by
faith the deep truths of the Lord's coming suffering, death and resurrection. Our Lord repeats these
deep truths immediately after this incidence, but
the disciples did not understand and were afraid to
ask Him questions about the truths (Mark 9:30–32).
Fundamentally, the faith of the disciples had not
grown much, for assuredly it was not the size of a
mustard seed yet.

The second ingredient of the failure of the nine
disciples was not being able to discern the nature
or depth of the problem, which Jesus refers to as
"this mountain." There are difficulties in life and
ministry that outwardly seem the same as before
or somewhat less complex; but with eyes of faith

looking to the Lord alone, one sees the complexity and the impossibility of the situation. The complexity can be as a result of an individual's background or upbringing, strained or awkward relationships with people, previous failures and so forth. In the world of demons, there are degrees of differences. In the age of complexity, there are degrees of complexity. In the world of the impossible, there are also degrees of differences. To cope with these kinds of mountains, one needs faith, discernment and prayer.

Jesus addresses the deficiency in the prayer life: "This kind cannot come out by anything but prayer." Past successes, the busyness of life or ministry, the apparent simplicity of the problem, the lack of discernment, the lack of perseverance in the spiritual disciplines of life (Bible study, prayer, fasting, etc.) or ineptness—or all of the above—undermine the prayer life of the believer and make him or her ineffective. For instance, if the problem is extremely difficult, one needs divine insight and discernment along with the Word of God to pray about the different parts of the problem (the seen and the unseen) and to know God's timeline about how to proceed. There is nothing too little to bring up before the Lord (Zechariah 4:10, "For who has despised the day of small things?"), no matter whether the smallness is related to the type of problem or the small parts of a very complex problem. Praying this way is a spiritual discipline that is in-

grained into the life along with a continual dependence upon Christ, His Spirit and the sword of the
Spirit. One of the reasons this kind of praying is not
ingrained into many believers' lives is that we see
our problems as one-dimensional and not multifac-
eted with many unseen subproblems or subissues.

All of the disciples had failed in faith, in discernment and in prayer. They had failed in the ideal environment on the mountaintop, and they had failed
in the valley of chaos, confusion and need. In each
of these places and in every other place, one needs
faith, discernment and prayer. However, two observations are critical here. First, the deep truths of
the Word need to be taught, for without them believers do not press on to maturity in Christ. Baby
food does not prepare the believer for the successes
and failures in life and ministry. Baby food from
the Scriptures does not train the heart or mind to
discern good and evil (Hebrews 5:14) and to understand the time lags between truth, its application or
nonapplication and divinely orchestrated events.
Second, let us not forget that our response to deep
truth from the lips of our Savior and Lord will impact our success or failure in the next crisis of life
or ministry. There will be a testing of the heart and
life to either show the quality of the heart as a result
of embracing the truth or the weakness and failure
of the heart as a result of ignoring the truth. When
tested, I pray that each of us will not be found wanting as the disciples were.

Life Response to Biblical Truth

1. Men and women will not trust God until they
    have to. They will trust in their past successes,
    in their organization, in their natural or spiri-
    tual gifts, in their training (spiritual, religious
    or worldly), in majorities or polls, in methods
    or in self as long as they can rather than trust
    God. One of the greatest misconceptions of the
    Christian life is that the believer wants to work
    it out and let God help rather than let God do
    His part and the believer participate with obe-
    dience in the power of the Holy Spirit in God's
    work. The Lord allowed these disciples to expe-
    rience humiliation, frustration, embarrassment,
    criticism and failure to empty them of pride and
    to cast out the demon of self-sufficiency. Only
    when God exposes our self-sufficiency, and we
    see that self-sufficiency as He sees it, can we be-
    gin to understand faith and how to respond by
    faith to the situations we find ourselves in. May
    we come to this realization quickly! However,
    we cannot come to this point by self-evaluation
    or self-effort or self-abasement. God must lead
    us there, and we must respond by faith to Him
    where and when He wants.

2. The lack of exercising faith in one instance pre-
    pares one to not exercise faith in the next in-
    stance in life. There is a progression in littleness
    of faith from the essentials of life to the battles
    in life. First, this progression begins in not trust-

ing God for food, clothing and shelter (Matthew 6:19–34), either in possessing these things or managing the things we do have. Second, littleness of faith in this realm spreads to not trusting His Word for direction and protection in the storms of life (Mark 4:35–41). These storms reveal our self-absorption and failure to pay close attention to His Word. Third, littleness of faith manifests itself in an unhealthy concern for the temporal, evidenced by blindness to God's ways and the inability to correlate God's works and words to our circumstances and times (Matthew 16; Mark 8). Finally, littleness of faith about the doctrines concerning the suffering, death and resurrection of our Lord will make us unfruitful and inept in the service of our Lord or in the spiritual battles that come our way.

Littleness of faith in any of these arenas equips us to respond in the future by the flesh. The flesh cannot please God so God in His great mercy intervenes in our lives to break this ungodly response by engineering situations that should force us to trust Him and not ourselves. What an awesome and loving God we should be serving!

3. We each need to be aware that the agonies of life are the plows that God uses to prepare the soil of our hearts to receive the Word with humility (James 1:21) and to enable us to respond in faith and total dependence on Him. We try

to avoid these agonies, to shorten them or to explain them away; but they are a vital part of God's plan that we should embrace as tools of God to correct or mend our faith, our mind and our hearts. Any other response may require us to experience such agonies again and again. May we be teachable and pliable in the hands of a loving, faithful God!

4. The disciples and the father were both lacking faith, but the disciples did not recognize their lack of faith, even though they were more mature spiritually and had spent more physical time with Jesus. On the other hand, the father did recognize his unbelief, yet he had not been the constant companion of Jesus.

There are two serious warnings that come from these events. First, knowledge makes arrogant or puffs up (1 Corinthians 8:1) and can seriously undermine our faith. We need to be like the psalmist who said, "I hastened and did not delay to keep Your commandments" (Psalm 119:60). When we ignore truth, delay in responding to truth or rationalize truth as appropriate for someone else but not us, we risk damaging our faith and our relationship with our Savior. Second, we all need reproving for our lack of faith at some point. The disciples and the father had Jesus, and we have His Word and the Holy Spirit to convict us of sin and righteousness and judgment (John 16:8). That can and should be sufficient, but we need to recognize that the heart can be so sick and deceived (Jeremiah 17:9). In that state, it may take the agonies of life to bring us to repentance. On the other hand, if we have cultivated strong biblical and accountable relationships such that we have given certain people the freedom to reprove us when our faith wanes or fails, then God may speak to us that way as well. Blessed is the individual that has such relationships! Start praying about finding them if you don't have such relationships.

5. In this chapter, we have seen from the Scriptures that just because someone is successful that is no guarantee that his or her success was done by faith in the power of the Holy Spirit. In this age of perpetuating programs, it is very likely that which was begun by faith is being perfected by the flesh. Perfection by the flesh does not lead to living by faith. In fact, we can find ourselves in the position that Samson was in that "he did not know that the LORD had departed from him" (Judges 16:20). Likewise, the disciples did not know why they could not cast the demon out. They had spent over two years with Jesus, they had previous successes in casting out demons, they had seen numerous miracles and they had heard great teaching; but they experienced failure nevertheless. At least they recognized that they should have succeeded

and wanted to know why they had not. They should be commended for that recognition, for that is a key step in learning to walk by faith.

On the other side of the coin, how can we tell if someone has walked by faith? We probably cannot unless we know the person intimately and understand his or her motives. "The LORD weighs the motives" (Proverbs 16:2), and He can reveal those motives as He sees fit. Ultimately, all such motives will be revealed at the judgment seat of God.

6. A real deficiency in our day is the lack of spiritual discernment. The disciples did not discern the complexities of the situation with the father's son. Likewise, as believers we do not discern the degrees of differences existing in today's problems. In the realm of demons, there are degrees of differences. In the complex world of relationships, there are degrees of differences. In the sphere of sickness, there are degrees of differences. In the domain of the impossible, there are also degrees of differences.

Some mountains are higher or more difficult to conquer than we could ever imagine unless we see them as the Father in heaven does. "The effective prayer of a righteous man can accomplish much" (James 5:16). But we have become too busy with life, with religion, with programs, with sports and with getting ahead; and we have become guilty of littleness of prayer. In his famous book, *Power Through Prayer*, E.M. Bounds said, "Of these two evils, perhaps little praying is worse than no praying. Little praying is a kind of make-believe, a salvo for the conscience, a farce, and a delusion."[4]

Both sets of disciples—the three on the mountaintop with Jesus and the nine in the valley—had prayed a little, but it was insufficient in light of the situations and complexities they faced. We too are guilty of such little praying! May God grant us discernment to see the complexities before us that we may realize quickly how much we need to pray to see the battles won and our faith matured.

Questions for Reflection

1. As noted, the agonies of life with health, children, jobs, family, relationships and more are the plows that God uses to prepare the soil of our heart. Can we soften the blows of such agonies, ignore them, sidestep them or run from them? What should our response be?

2. Failure in a venture or situation is probably a stronger teacher than success. What have you learned about yourself and about God in your past failures?

3. How are faith, prayer and discernment related? Why is the lack of discernment these days a troubling sign?

4. The interrelationship between success and faith and between failure and faith has frequently been distorted or misinterpreted. Why is this distortion or misinterpretation so dangerous?

5. Without experiencing failure, we will have a warped perspective of God. What does this mean to us as individuals or members of a biblical ministry?

6. We cannot ride on the coattails of previous successes we have had or others have had. Why is that so critical to us in walking by faith in God?

7. The father's faith was influenced by the long-term difficulties with his son and the failure of the nine disciples. How has your faith been affected by long-term trials or by the weaknesses or failures in others? What is the solution?

Chapter 9

The Request to Increase My Faith

Read Luke 17:1–19

While our Lord is winding down His ministry on His final journey to Jerusalem, the Gospel of Luke (17:5) records an interesting request from the lips of the apostles to our Lord: "Increase our faith!" The Lord had been teaching on faith and recognizing the faith of individuals for two years. Faith and the basics of life were taught in the Sermon on the Mount. The great faith of the centurion and the Syrophoenician woman were recognized and commended. Faith and the storms of life were correlated. Faith and its stages were noted, and the disciples were reprimanded on numerous occasions for their lack or littleness of faith. Thus, it seems strange that after two years, the apostles ask Jesus for increased faith as if there is a magic formula to so do. Let's look at the events around this request to understand the Lord's answer.

Precipitating Events for a Petition for More Faith

Many Bible commentators see the events and discussions recorded in Luke chapter 17 as disjointed or disconnected. However, that is really not the case! The words of Jesus in Luke 17:1–4 to His disciples on stumbling blocks precipitate the petition for increased faith from the apostles:

> He said to His disciples, "It is inevitable that stumbling blocks come, but woe to him through whom they come! It would be better for him if a millstone were hung around his neck and he were thrown into the sea, than that he would cause one of these little ones to stumble. Be on your guard! If your brother sins, rebuke him; and if he repents, forgive him. And if he sins against you seven times a day, and returns to you seven times, saying, 'I repent,' forgive him."

The phrase "stumbling block" refers to anything that would cause another believer to fall by the wayside or that would become a hindrance to his or her faith. As long as this world is ruled by the Prince of Darkness, Jesus says that stumbling blocks will be inevitable. On the other hand, just because they are inevitable does not mean that we should fear them. We should always be on guard or on watch for stumbling blocks or temptations to sin because we cannot let down our guard in the power of the Holy Spirit for a minute.

Jesus hints at two ways to avoid the complications of stumbling blocks. First, if a brother or sister in Christ has damaged the overall good of God's work, he or she should be rebuked. The Scriptures (Matthew 18:15–20; 1 Corinthians 5:9–13) talk of church discipline with the following order: (a) personal reprimand in private, (b) elder or group reproof, (c) reproof from the church and (d) exclusion from the church fellowship. To not take the appropriate disciplinary action not only hurts the one who sinned, but it also does not cause others to fear sin and its consequences. We all sin, but some sins we rationalize away. Sometimes our heart is so hard that we don't see sin. For instance, if an individual believer is gossiping about or slandering another, that person should be confronted or disciplined. The win-win is that a believer is restored to the Lord, the body of Christ is uplifted and protected and church leadership is perfected in personal relationships. Proverbs says, "Better is open rebuke than love that is concealed" (27:5).

The second key to avoiding the complications of stumbling blocks is forgiveness. If one forgives another and the individual turns from his or her sin back to God, one has restored or gained a brother or sister. If one forgives another and that individual repents but keeps returning to the sin, we must be careful to forgive him or her. Lack of forgiveness on our part could be a stumbling block for us, the repeat offender or others who are observing the process. An unforgiving, legalistic spirit keeps track of wrongs; and a prideful, unforgiving spirit boasts about someone else's sin not having a grip on their life. There is no way to increase faith when we have constraints or limitations on our forgiveness toward others (and even ourselves).

Petition for Faith

After these instructions from Jesus on helping others who sin and forgiving others who sin against you, the disciples recognized how hard it is to restore a brother or sister in Christ who has stumbled in the faith and how hard it is to habitually forgive another. It was beyond their human ability! The short petition for faith and part of the Lord's answer follows: "The apostles said to the Lord, 'Increase our faith!' And the Lord said, 'If you had faith like a mustard seed, you would say to this mulberry tree, "Be uprooted and be planted in the sea;" and it would obey you'" (Luke 17:5–6).

The disciples ask Jesus to increase their faith to deal with such situations, once and for all. They did not ask for increased love though love is foundational to forgiveness. They asked for faith because by faith we must love in difficult circumstances.

The disciples recognized that faith was necessary for them to trust God for the consequences of relationships, to resolve hard feelings, to clear up misunderstandings, to bring glory to God and to work for the good of all parties involved. The disciples immediately knew that this was more faith than they had. It takes faith to reprimand a wayward brother or sister in love just as it takes faith to continually forgive a habitually sinning brother or sister in Christ.

In passing, it is important to point out that our disposition to reprimand or to forgive is frequently nested in our spiritual gifts. For instance, a believer with prophetic gifts might find it easier to reprimand another brother or sister, but it must still be done by faith with the right words and the right timing. On the other hand, a believer with mercy gifts might find it easier to forgive (this forgiveness must also be by faith and not by human strength) and very difficult to reprimand or correct another believer. Thus, no matter what spiritual gifts or natural dispositions we possess, we must be obedient to the Word of God and the stirrings of the Holy Spirit in relationships with others, whether confrontation or forgiveness is required.

Our Lord's answer to their request for increased faith seems strange. "If you had faith like a mustard seed, you would say to this mulberry tree, 'Be uprooted and be planted in the sea,' and it would obey you." If they had faith? Of course they did. The apostles had healed the sick and cast out demons. Peter had walked on water. Yet they did not have as much faith as a mustard seed after two years with Jesus! Having faith needs an object. Many people have faith in doctors, mechanics, pilots and so on; but the object of our faith should constantly be God. Having faith in God must be in harmony with God's will, God's Word and God's glory. If it is God's will to cast this mountain (this obstacle or difficulty standing in your way) or that mulberry tree (a deep-rooted difficulty) into the sea, then those things are possible.

Within any body of believers there can be many mountains and deep-rooted problems that should be cast into the sea to preserve the unity of the body and to aid the growth of individual believers as well as the corporate growth of believers. In dealing with insurmountable difficulties, one does not need great faith in God but rather faith in a great God. Our perspective of God must be greater and more expansive than ever before. When that happens, no matter what the size of our faith, we will see great things done by even a greater God. That should be our focus.

Prescription for Success in Faith

Jesus gently reprimanded the apostles, saying that great faith was not required in order to forgive others. He then offered a parable to emphasize his point:

> Which of you, having a slave plowing or tending sheep, will say to him when he has come in from the field, "Come immediately and sit down to eat"? But will he

not say to him, "Prepare something for me to eat, and properly clothe yourself and serve me while I eat and drink; and afterward you may eat and drink"? He does not thank the slave because he did the things which were commanded, does he? So you too, when you do all the things which are commanded you, say, "We are unworthy slaves; we have done only that which we ought to have done." (Luke 17:7–10)

In this parable, Jesus gives the prescription for increased faith in obedience and attitude. The setting for the parable is a master who only has or can only afford one slave, who does all the plowing, shepherding, cooking, waiting on tables and anything else. One might say that this servant is a jack-of-all-trades.

Jesus asks three questions in the parable. First, is any master going to tell his slave who has worked all day to immediately come in and eat without taking care of the master's desires? The answer is obvious! Obedience and responsibility to the Master of all does not end at a certain time of the day but continues until His desires are met. Each day is another opportunity to walk in obedience to the Master of all. Second, is not the master going to prioritize the servant's duties with those of the master first and of the servant second? The answer again is obvious! The will of the Father or the Son always takes precedence over the will or desires of the servant. The servant must always be in tune to the voice of the Father for the priorities of the day. And third, is any master going to thank the servant for doing what he was commanded or expected to do? Obviously, the answer is still no! The servant was bought with a very precious price so he must strive to be faithful in what the Master of all has commanded him to do. That faithfulness should not expect or demand a reward, even in thankfulness. Such faithfulness will be rewarded in God's time on earth or in heaven when He says, "Well done, good and faithful slave" (Matthew 25:21).

Thus far, the essence of this parable is that obedience is a continuum. It is not occasional, single acts over a lifetime, but daily steps on a long journey to Christ-likeness in mind-set, behavior, focus on others, prayer and doing the will of the Father unbegrudgingly. For the apostles and for us today, there will be easy, difficult and extremely difficult, if not almost impossible, situations in ministry. There are tasks that no one wants to do, tasks requiring time, energy and involvement. The very difficult task of rebuking a brother or sister in Christ, for example, is not something anyone wants to do; but we must be obedient in the power of the Holy Spirit to do these tasks even when they come at the end of a busy day of service.

The second part of the prescription for increased faith is a proper attitude of humility. Just because 99.9% of believers do not obey the Word of God in certain areas of confrontation, forgiveness or stumbling blocks does not mean special thanks or reward from the Father goes to those who do. Most believers even today as in Jesus' day feel that much service to God or much obedience is worthy of reward or recognition. It is easy to get trapped by thinking that if we obey God in this area of life, then He owes us. God is never placed in our debt by our obedience. We are forever in His debt! "Yet for your sake He became poor, so that you through His poverty might become rich" (2 Corinthians 8:9). Our motive or attitude for obedience should not be reward or recognition but to please the Master of all and to bring glory to His name. We are "unworthy" or unprofitable or useless servants. Apart from the work of God in the power of the Holy Spirit in our lives and the circumstances around us, we can do nothing (John 15:5). We need to see ourselves and God properly, which means that we need to clothe ourselves with humility toward one another and humble ourselves under the hand of God (1 Peter 5:1–7).

Portrait of Increased Faith

While journeying to Jerusalem, somewhere in the area between Samaria and Galilee, and shortly after the request for "increased faith" from the apostles, Jesus receives a request from ten lepers for mercy. Some might contend that this event is not related to the request for increased faith, but faith is a critical element of this miracle, especially for one Samaritan. The miracle is recorded in the Gospel of Luke:

While He was on the way to Jerusalem, He was passing between Samaria and Galilee. As He entered a village, ten leprous men who stood at a distance met Him; and they raised their voices, saying, "Jesus, Master, have mercy on us!" When He saw them, He said to them, "Go and show yourselves to the priests." And as they were going, they were cleansed. Now one of them, when he saw that he had been healed, turned back, glorifying God with a loud voice, and he fell on his face at His feet, giving thanks to Him. And he was a Samaritan. Then Jesus answered and said, "Were there not ten cleansed? But the nine—where are they? Was no one found who returned to give glory to God, except this foreigner?" And He said to him, "Stand up and go; your faith has made you well." (17:11–19)

There are four parts to this specific miracle that provide insight to the increased faith of the Samaritan:

1. **Request for mercy from all**. The ten lepers, obedient to the law, stood at a distance and voiced their cry for mercy in unison. By this time, everyone was aware of Christ's miracles. Thirty of the thirty-five recorded miracles had occurred prior to this event, and Jesus had not failed once. Did their request for mercy show faith in Jesus? It probably did not, and their response to His words revealed the extent of that faith.

2. **Remedy from Jesus**. Their loud voices in unison must have captured His attention. The Lord did not ask them what their request was, for

He had already heard it. When He saw them or when the eyes of God probed the hearts and minds of these ten lepers, He spoke His remedy from a distance: "Go and show yourselves to the priests." As the ten lepers took the steps of faith and obedience, they were cleansed. One can almost visualize the Lord's eyes following the ten lepers as they headed to the priests for a unique testimony that "the kingdom of God was in their midst."

3. **Response of the Samaritan**. When the Samaritan was healed, he returned to see the Healer Himself face-to-face. The Samaritan returned glorifying God with a loud voice, probably as loud as the original request for mercy. In addition, he worshipped at our Lord's feet (humility), giving thanks to Him.

4. **Retort of the Lord.** Where the other nine were was the question of Jesus. Ten had been healed, but only one returned to give glory to God. Ten had faith and experienced the benefit of healing, but only one had more faith and got to know his Benefactor face-to-face. This Samaritan got to look in the eyes of the One who saw all and knew all. He got the privilege to hear specific instructions again from the lips of our Lord, "Rise, and go your way; your faith has made you well."

The response of the Samaritan shows the increased faith of a true disciple. It was the response of obedience, initiative, thanksgiving, humility and waiting for further specific instructions. Tozer once said that "faith engages God, the one great Reality, who gave and gives existence to all things."[1] The other nine lepers displayed faith in Jesus' words, but this Samaritan leper was the only one who did what he ought to have done: give thanks. The Samaritan went further in faith as he sought to be engaged with God face-to-face. The joy of obedience in a task or from a benefit passes with time, but continually being at the feet of Jesus to hear His words and to give thanks lasts a lifetime.

The ten lepers had exhibited faith with their obedience to Jesus' words, but the Samaritan leper showed increased faith as he came back to thank Jesus. Likewise, those believers today wanting increased faith must keep coming back to Jesus as the Samaritan did for there is no onetime, magic formula for increased faith.

Life Response to Biblical Truth

1. God does not want us to get stagnant in the life of faith. In 1 John 2:13–14, the Apostle John, under the inspiration of the Holy Spirit, mentions three levels of maturity: children, young men and fathers. These same three levels could be deduced from Titus 2:3–5 in terms of children, young women and older women. All three lev-

els know the Father and have experienced for-giveness for sin, but nothing else is said about the child level. The young men or women are strong, have the Word of God abiding in them, and have overcome the evil one. These young men or women are exhibiting faith in action in the battles of life and ministry. The comment about the fathers (older women) is that they "know Him who has been from the beginning." They have progressed in their faith to a point that they are mentoring and discipling oth-ers who in turn are teaching others (2 Timothy 2:2) while maintaining a deep communion with Him who has always been. Their faith is ever increasing as they desire to engage with God each day and each moment. There is no magic formula for such a faith journey as the apostles needed to understand. It takes time, divinely or-dained events and the biblical response to such events to have our faith grow.

2. There are combinations of precipitating events in the life of each believer that boxes them in without any solutions or options. The disciples had been with Jesus for at least two years and had experienced some unique precipitating events, such as the storm at sea and failure in the valley of ministry in casting out a demon. However, for some reason these frightening and humbling experiences had not awakened the chord of faith in God that they should have had.

Likewise today, we believers will be blindsided by difficult precipitating events and be unable to see God behind them for the sake of our weak faith in Him. In that light, it is no wonder that our loving Father allows other precipitating events to break us, humble us, teach us and bring us to the end of our self-effort. If we respond correctly, these events will be critical in conforming us to Christ and in jumpstarting our faith. Without these divine precipitating events, however, our faith would become more stagnant, and that is not God's desire for His people.

3. God, in His omniscience, knows the types and timings of precipitating events we each need to be awakened in faith. There is tremendous comfort in realizing that the types, timing, sequences and intensity of such precipitating events have been divinely ordained for us. What a loving God we have the privilege of serving and knowing! Certain events, such as confrontation, forgiveness of a habitual offender or extremely difficult trials, can end up causing our faith to blossom or to droop. If our faith fails in the situation, you can be sure that our Father in heaven will return us to the same point again sometime in the future. We each need to realize that there is no magic formula in these situations—other than to cling to God by setting deep roots into the Scriptures, spending time in prayer, listening

for His voice and being obedient in the normal course of everyday events and relationships.

4. The disciples exhibited faith on some occasions, but the continuum of walking by faith was not there as evidenced by our Lord's gentle reprimand on several occasions for the littleness or lack of faith. They finally saw their inability and God's power properly. Now, one might try to make the case that they didn't have the Holy Spirit yet, so consequently their sluggish faith is understandable. They also didn't have the New Testament at that time. What they did have, however, was the physical presence of the Living Word continually with them. What is our excuse? We have the Holy Spirit residing within us, and we have the complete Scriptures. Is it that we have no models of living by faith today? On the contrary, an in-depth look into the Gospels and the Old Testament will reveal many examples of faith. Paul wrote, "For whatever was written in earlier times was written for our instruction, so that through perseverance and the encouragement of the Scriptures we might have hope" (Romans 15:4). May we be students of the Scriptures in the power of the Holy Spirit!

5. Is it wrong to ask for increased faith as the apostles did? Jesus didn't overtly correct them for asking, but He did instruct them that there is no

magic formula for faith to be increased quickly or long-term. As believers, we need to do what we ought to do in accordance to the Word of God, in the power of the Spirit. The faith of a believer progresses as he stays engaged with the God of all and walks in obedience to Him daily. It is in the rut of daily life at the office, home, store, club and in the way we use our time that faith is refined by our obedience to the Father. There are no shortcuts in increasing one's faith. The apostles' motives for asking for increased faith bypassed God's plan for how faith is increased. They were looking for a shortcut, but there is none! The writer of Hebrews gives some insight into this divine plan when he said, "[Jesus] learned obedience from the things which He suffered" (Hebrews 5:8). Clearly, suffering as well as trials (James 1:2–4) are things that God uses to mold our faith. Will we have situations of suffering and trials where we may need faith to endure and to respond in a way that God is glorified? Certainly! Should one feel awkward or less than spiritual to ask for faith in a difficult or confusing situation? Certainly not! As noted in Hebrews 11:6, "Without faith it is impossible to please Him, for he who comes to God must believe that He is and that He is a rewarder of those who seek Him." To please God it takes faith, but the essence of that faith is nurtured as we engage God daily, in person and through the Scriptures. We will need divine wisdom by faith, divine strength by faith and divine encouragement to stay the course by faith. Each precipitating event ordained by God will require us to cling to Him and ask Him for the requisite faith to be in daily dependence for there is no onetime prayer for increased faith!

6. Finally, so far as we can tell from the Bible, the Samaritan is the only one of the ten who had increased faith. The ten lepers were all obedient to the words of Jesus. As they were obedient by faith, they were all healed. Yet only the Samaritan came back to engage the Savior face-to-face with humility, worship and thanksgiving. In that engagement with Jesus, his faith was increased. He knelt at His feet, listened to His voice, heard His questions and received His commands; and he went away more changed than the other nine.

May we come to the Savior daily as the Samaritan did so that the by-product of that daily engagement with Jesus Christ will be increased faith. Could the story of the ten lepers indicate that only one in ten believers desires an increased faith? If so, may you be that one!

Questions for Reflection

1. The Scriptures, as discussed in this chapter, have re-
    vealed that there is no magic formula for increased
    faith or no "quickie" for getting more faith. Can you
    list or share with someone else the events or situa-
    tions that God has used to increase your faith in Him
    over recent weeks, months or years?

2. What was it about these sovereign precipitating
    events that affected your faith? The uniqueness of
    the event? The timing of the event? The intensity of
    the event? Why is giving thanks to God so critical
    with such precipitating events?

3. We frequently place constraints on our forgiveness
    toward others, such as if so-and-so does such-and-
    such, then I will forgive. Or we say that we will for-
    give in our way and in our time. What is the impact
    on our faith with such constraints on forgiveness?

4. Increased faith seems to be nourished from daily
    obedience to the Word of God and in humility to-
    ward God and others. As such, there is a daily de-
    pendence upon God. Can you briefly voice to God

or others what that walk of faith has been like for the last twenty-four hours? List it on paper or voice it verbally to someone else who might need that encouragement.

5. The Samaritan recognized his wretched condition and was not content with it. Do you desire to engage God day by day and to please Him in all that you do? Do you recognize the ways that the Father draws you to Himself? How does James 4:8 ("Draw near to God and He will draw near to you") describe our responsibility?

6. Sometimes, we must "love by faith." What is the meaning of that phrase? For instance, how do you love the "takers," the "schemers," the "lepers of our day" and the "drainers" of life? Recount some events where you had to "love by faith."

Chapter 10

Will He Find Faith?

Read Luke 18:1–8

Since the Sermon on the Mount, all of the inter-actions about faith sprang out of events where the disciples were present. In these events, either the disciples failed to exercise faith or someone else exhibited great faith, and these extremes provided the opportunity for our Lord to communicate some deep truths about living by faith. This next discussion on matters of faith came after a discourse with the disciples on "the last days" and a parable about prayer.

The discourse with the disciples about the "end times" addressed believers' longing to see the days of the Son of Man, but they would not see it. But first the suffering of the Son of Man had to occur, along with rejection by His generation. Second, in the days of Noah, when only a remnant of six exhibited faith and where the rest of the world was eating, drinking, marrying and being given in marriage, there was judgment and destruction from a worldwide flood. The biblical description of the world at the time of the flood was as follows:

> Then the LORD saw that the wickedness of man was great on the earth, and that every intent of the thoughts of his heart was only evil continually. The LORD was sorry that He had made man on the earth, and He was grieved in His heart. The LORD said, "I will blot out man whom I have created from the face of the land, from man to animals to creeping things and to birds of the sky; for I am sorry that I have made them." But Noah found favor in the eyes of the LORD. These are the records of the generations of Noah. Noah was a righteous man, blameless in his time; Noah walked with God. . . . Now the earth was corrupt in the sight of God, and the earth was filled with violence. God looked on the earth, and behold, it was corrupt; for all flesh had corrupted their way upon the earth. (Genesis 6:5–9, 11–12)

Likewise, in the time of Lot, who had faith but whose righteous soul was tormented day after day with the lawless deeds of the people of Sodom and Gomorrah, judgment came again, but this time with fire and brimstone. Lot's faith was weak as displayed by his hesitation about the judgment of the city (Genesis 19:15) and the need to remove him from Sodom by angelic force. The biblical description of Sodom and Gomorrah comes best from Genesis 19:5, which shows the homosexuality that permeated that society. "And they called to Lot and said to him, 'Where are the men who came to you tonight? Bring them out to us that we may have relations with them'" (Genesis 19:5). However, the passage in Ezekiel 16:49 reveals even more depths of sin with pride, abundant food and careless ease with no help for the poor and needy: "Behold, this was the guilt of your sister Sodom: she and her daughters had arrogance, abundant food and careless ease, but she did not help the poor and needy" (Ezekiel 16:49). These two passages reveal the extreme wickedness of Sodom and Gomorrah and why God judged them.

No matter if the sin was worldwide or local, we see four obvious issues. First, there was acceleration or an exponential growth of sin at its worst in the society or cultures at those times. It contaminated the reasoning, the actions and the treatment of others, and it precluded a proper value of things eternal. Second, the flourishing of evil would affect God's people in the future. Third, the remnant that lived by faith was small. At the time of Noah, there were only six. At the time of Lot, there were only three saved by angelic force from destruction. The faithful remnant has always been small. This discourse eventually leads to the ending question in Luke 18:8, "When the Son of Man comes, will He find faith on the earth?" And four, there will be a judgment of evil and a deliverance of God's chosen ones. It will come, but meanwhile God's remnant must persevere by faith!

Preview of Prayer Priorities

With the backdrop of the "end times" discussion from the 17th chapter of Luke being a fresh fragrance in the air, Jesus begins telling a parable. The parable is addressed to "them" and the closest antecedent to this "them" is the disciples in Luke 17:22. What our Lord had to say to the disciples are things that we need to hear today as well: "Now He was telling them a parable to show that at all times they ought to pray and not to lose heart" (Luke 18:1).

The first priority from Luke 18:1 is that God's people should or ought to pray at all times. The Apostle Paul picks up this same priority when he encourages the saints to "pray without ceasing" (1 Thessalonians 5:17) or to "pray at all times in the Spirit" (Ephesians 6:18). This praying is not to be only occasional, or just in difficult times, but at all times. These times would cover when things are going well, so-so and not going well in any way. To pray only in difficult times is to miss the fellowship, praise, confession and thanksgiving that should characterize the majority of our prayers. Supplication for help should be a small portion of our prayer life.

Is it possible for one to pray at all times or without ceasing? The answer is "yes," and the key is found in Paul's letter to the Ephesians when he says to "pray at all times in the Spirit." As one walks moment-by-moment in the power of the Holy Spirit, the fellowship with the Father is not broken; and one can pray to the Father about anything within a split second. For instance, one might praise God for the beautiful sunrise on the way to work, for providing for the birds sitting on a high telephone wire, for eyes to see opportunities to make a difference in someone else's life and so forth. This kind of continual praying is like natural breathing.

If one only prays when there is a felt need or when times are difficult, then our prayers are filled with supplication and not the other ingredients. Since it is very likely that most Christians associate rich fellowship with the Father only with hard times, it takes difficult times to move us into a stronger fellowship with Him. What God desires, though, is for us to pray at all times. That heavenly desire is not about continually asking Him for things but a two-way fellowship that is indescribably rich. It is the deepest and most enjoyable conversation between friends. Jesus said the same: "You are My friends if you do what I command you" (John 15:14). Prayer is at its best when it is the total expression of a life of obedience as one carries his or her own cross.

To pray at only certain times is to not cultivate the habit of praying at all times. This is a spiritual discipline that takes time, effort and assessment. Our pace of life in the Western world does not provide much time for reflective praying. We may need to carve time out early in the morning, with prayer breaks or prayer moments throughout the day. Time and effort empowered by the Holy Spirit will be needed. More important is the assessment of our praying at all times: Is my praying in a rut? Am I praying about the same things all of the time? Are my prayers filled only with petitions? Many times it takes some taxing or precipitating event to force us to evaluate our prayer life. On the other hand, if we are praying at all times, there should be frequent assessment of our prayer quality under the power of the Holy Spirit, not in the power of the flesh with condemnation.

The second priority in prayer is to not lose heart. Paul talks about not losing heart in the ministry of the gospel in his second letter to the Corinthians (4:1), about not losing heart with the decay of outer man and the renewal of the inner man (4:16), about not losing heart in doing good (Galatians 6:9) and about not losing heart in tribulation or trials (Ephesians 3:13). Ministry among people and by the power of the Holy Spirit is not always successful. Some couples, whom we have counseled, still went ahead and got divorces. Individuals we have discipled for years still go astray and become unfruitful. There are hills and valleys, blessings and discouragement. The low times in the valleys will seem to be the larger part of ministry many times; but if our eyes are always on our Savior as we leave the results to Him and His timing, we will not lose heart. The decay of the outer man and the renewal of the inner man can also be discouraging, but we will not lose heart if we consider Him faithful as He transforms us into the image of Christ.

Lastly, trials or tribulations also cause us to lose heart as we don't understand why something has happened. Sometimes, with time, we can reflect back and partially see what God did, but again we must focus on our loving God and realize by faith that what He is doing is for our best.

When there is no obvious fruit from ministry, when well doing is laborious, when the decay of the outer man seems to be getting greater, when trials are multiplying or when praying seems to be useless, it is human nature to lose heart. However, by faith we need to realize that there will be fruit from it all in God's time. Maybe that fruit will not be seen until heaven, but one thing is sure—that the God who made us and redeemed us has allowed these unfruitful situations to occur to drive us to a greater dependence upon Him. It takes faith to persevere in prayer, in ministry, in well doing, in trials and through outer decay, especially when the results are not evident or they are delayed a long time. That type of faith sees God as great, as in control and as working out all things for His glory.

Persistence in Asking

To pray at all times implies a dependence upon the Father and to do so without losing heart when nothing seems to be moving in a positive direction implies a helplessness nestled in the arms of our loving God. This childlike trust and helplessness is reflected in the words of the psalmist:

> O LORD, my heart is not proud, nor my eyes haughty; nor do I involve myself in great matters, or in things too difficult for me. Surely I have composed and quieted my soul; like a weaned child rests against his mother, my soul is like a weaned child within me (Psalm 131:1–2).

To illustrate the realities of this kind of trust and faith, Jesus proceeds to tell a parable about a widow and a judge. The parables Jesus relates in the Gospels are not just isolated stories; instead they were communicated to answer a question or drive home a point. The points in this case were the interrelationships among perseverance, prayer and faith. In addition, parables were an easy way to remember the truths that were veiled to the unbelieving and revealed to the saints. This one is about the wicked judge and the widow:

> Now He was telling them a parable to show that at all times they ought to pray and not to lose heart, saying, "In a certain city there was a judge who did not fear God and did not respect man. There was a widow in that city, and she kept coming to him, saying, 'Give me legal protection from my opponent.' For a while he

was unwilling; but afterward he said to himself, 'Even though I do not fear God nor respect man, yet because this widow bothers me, I will give her legal protection, otherwise by continually coming she will wear me out." (Luke 18:1–5)

The three characters in the parable are the wicked judge, the widow and an opponent. The easiest way to understand the complete essence of this parable is to do a contrast as delineated in Table 10.1.

Table 10.1—Comparisons in the Parable with What Scripture Says about God and the Elect

Parable	Scripture elsewhere
Worldly, wicked judge	Good, gracious God
Unwilling judge	God willing to hear and act in His time
Judge-No fear of God (vertical)	God loves us
Judge-No respect of man (horizontal)	God wants the best for us
Judge-Selfish/unrighteous	God is righteous
Widow had wicked opponent	God's elect have Satan as adversary
Widow was weak	God's children are weak
Widow was helpless	God's elect are helpless unless clinging to the Father
Widow had a legitimate need	God's children have legitimate needs
Widow had a right	The elect have rights/claims from the promises of God
Widow was persistent	The elect must be persistent

There are three phases of contrast in this parable: the worldly, wicked judge versus our good and
gracious God; the wicked opponent of the widow
versus our opponent, Satan; and the weak widow
versus God's elect who are also weak. This wicked
judge is described as unwilling, self-sufficient and
with no fear or respect of God or man. This judge
has no concern for vertical or horizontal relationships. Our God is completely opposite in that He
hears our prayers, He acts in His time for our best
and He is very concerned about our relationship
with Him and with others. The character of our
God is one of love, omniscience, righteousness,
holiness, omnipotence and justness. He is not inconvenienced by our asking from the position of a
legitimate need. This first phase of contrast reveals
that the wicked judge and our gracious God are opposite extremes.

The second phase of contrast is that the woman
had an opponent or adversary just as God's people
have an adversary. The word for "opponent" is the
same word used in 1 Peter 5:8 for adversary: "Your
adversary, the devil, prowls around like a roaring
lion, seeking someone to devour." The woman's
opponent was real just like the saints' opponent,
the devil, is real. The woman needed legal protection from this ruthless opponent who was taking
advantage of widows, and under the law widows
and orphans were entitled to that legal protection.
But she had no advocate since her husband was

dead. In addition, the judge was indifferent to her cry for help. In contrast, our God is not indifferent, and He is not surprised by our circumstances. He will act in His time when we are where we need to be for His power to be manifested and for Him to receive all of the glory.

The third phase of the contrast is the widow and God's children, both of whom are weak. The widow was helpless, with no advocate or husband, with a legitimate need for protection and with a right to ask for that protection. God's children are also helpless and weak, but they frequently don't see themselves in such light. Believers have an Advocate with the Father (1 John 2:1), Jesus Christ; but most don't avail themselves of this opportunity with regularity. God's people definitely have needs and a right to ask for assistance in light of those needs, but they may not know their rights in light of the promises of God. This widow was persistent in the midst of her helplessness, her unmet need, her right to ask, her lack of an advocate and her opposition. She got what she asked for from this unrighteous judge, who responded to her to minimize his own inconvenience. God's children should also be persistent in asking for protection in their unique situations, and we can be sure that our God is not inconvenienced by such asking that is grounded in the Scriptures. However, as shall be noted, that persistence or faith is lacking today!

Perspectives of Persevering Prayer

The Lord in His graciousness does not leave the hearer of this parable hanging. He adds some parenthetical comments (Luke 18:6–8) to give clarity to the truths and their importance to the disciples and us today:

> And the Lord said, "Hear what the unrighteous judge said; now, will not God bring about justice for His elect who cry to Him day and night, and will He delay long over them? I tell you that He will bring about justice for them quickly. However, when the Son of Man comes, will He find faith on the earth?"

Jesus' parenthetical comments begin with what the unrighteous judge said about the widow bothering him and wearing him out with her continually asking. It is very evident that this judge was selfish as he sought to take care of the problem to get rid of the inconvenience. Our God is not like this wicked judge. He is not selfish, cannot be moved by nagging and cannot be manipulated. He is perfect, righteous, holy, omniscient, omnipresent, love, true, omnipotent, free, infinite and eternal, immutable and sovereign. None of these divine attributes describes this judge in the parable.

Our perfect Father knows what is to be before it happens, and He has the power to provide for what is to be changed or to be endured. Beyond this, He has a perfect time for it to happen. He is not surprised by our circumstances or situations. In fact, they have been sovereignly filtered through His loving hands to accomplish His purposes in our lives for being conformed more into the image of Jesus Christ. It seems from the words of Jesus that one of the greatest underminings of our faith is that we do not see God as He really is, but we see Him as someone from our past with all of his or her imperfections. The perfect perspective of our perfect Lord God comes from the Scriptures and our excelling daily relationship with our Friend and Savior as we see through His eyes.

Day and night, the Lord hears our cries for help. These calls for help have not been missed! However, there is a perfect time and a perfect way to meet these needs, and there is always divine purpose in God's delay in answering prayer. Maybe the purpose is to develop our persistence or faith, or to mold our prayers so that they are based more on the Word of God. Maybe it is to move us into a richer relationship with the Father or to affect others who are involved in or watching our circumstances. Will He delay long? No, the Father will delay only as long as necessary to accomplish His purposes. There is a perfect time and a perfect way to accomplish His perfect purposes. Christians must realize this if we want to excel in faith!

Jesus said that God will bring about justice for His children speedily. What is speedily? Is it in my timetable, or is it the same timetable that was evident in another believer's life? Or is it in God's timetable? We tend to seize on this word "speedily" or "quickly" meaning that the answer is coming soon. However, in light of the time spectrum of eternity, "speedily" may not even be in our lifetime.

Finally, "When the Son of Man comes, will He find faith on the earth?" Embodied in this question is the fact that our Lord is perfect, His timing and ways are perfect, His return will be perfect and His expectations about faith are perfect. Our Lord is coming again, like a thief in the night for His children (1 Thessalonians 4 and 5), and then later with all the signs and wonders at the end of the tribulation. The day of His return will be perfect, and only the perfect Father knows that day. Jesus' question ("Will He find faith on the earth?") seems to suggest that there will not be many walking by faith when He does return (a small remnant), as illustrated in the times of Noah (who had strong faith) and Lot (who had weak faith). Faith is not something that can be turned on like a water faucet. It is something that is cultivated in a life of obedience to the Scriptures as a believer walks in the power of the Holy Spirit.

If Jesus Christ were to return tomorrow, would there be evidence of walking by faith in our lives? Would the answer of most of us be "no"?

Life Response to Biblical Truth
1. There has always been a remnant of the faithful. Yet the wickedness in the world, in our culture,

in our society, in our locality and even in our families affects God's people. Unless the Lord God intervenes as He has done in the past or provides supernatural enablement or protection for the elect, they too could be sucked into the vortex of wickedness and sin. Our best protection today is to walk by faith in all we do, being obedient to the Scriptures and depending upon God's power from the Holy Spirit. In addition, we must be faithful to disciple the next generation, consisting of our physical children and our spiritual children. We must tutor them in the ways of faith so as to avoid "another generation after them who did not know the LORD, nor yet the work which He had done for Israel" (Judges 2:10).

2. "At all times they ought to pray" were the words of Jesus Himself. For most believers, the reality of those words in our experience seems to be impossible. Obedience to these words of Jesus is in fact impossible—in the power of the flesh. That is why the restatement of the Apostle Paul, "Pray at all times in the Spirit" (Ephesians 6:18), reveals that the power to keep this command comes from God Himself. As one walks in the power of the Holy Spirit and realizes that his or her sin grieves the Spirit, then the tendency is to deal with sin quickly so that fellowship with the Father is never broken or interrupted very long. This is critical to developing a disciplined

lifestyle of praying about all things at all times. However, this disciplined lifestyle of praying is not burdensome since it springs out of His love for us and our love for Him. It is like the open communications between friends. "You are My friends if you do what I command you" (John 15:14).

3. We know from the Scriptures that there are five things that may cause us to lose heart: ministering the gospel, doing well towards others, decaying of the outer man, enduring trials and praying. However, praying is the most important because it is in praying that we acknowledge our helplessness to do the other four. In praying, we acknowledge the need for empowerment and godly perspectives in pressing on with what our God has called us each to do with the gospel, in doing good toward others, in coping with our outer decay and with persevering in trials. When our complete helplessness is voiced to God, when we verbalize our praise of God's total sufficiency and when we take our stand on the promises of God, we will see God answer in His way and His time.

4. I wonder if our losing heart in prayer is not because of difficult circumstances that seem to be getting worse but because of our focus in these difficult times. Is it possible that my prayer life is very me-focused as I continually ask for things

for myself and for those around me? Is it possible that my prayers are short of praise and the heavenly perspective? Have I forgotten Jesus' words in Matthew 5:48: "Therefore you are to be perfect, as your heavenly Father is perfect"? Should not our perfect Lord, His perfect timing, His perfect ways, His perfect return, His perfect expectations, His perfect Word and the total perfection in the Trinity humble and encourage us no matter what? His delay or slowness in answering our prayers may be His work in our lives to force us to cling to Him and His Word, to develop endurance or persistence in us and to mold and make our faith in Him deeper than it would ever be without these trials. "That the proof of your faith, being more precious than gold which is perishable, even though tested by fire, may be found to result in praise and glory and honor at the revelation of Jesus Christ" (1 Peter 1:7).

5. To have the faith that God wants us to have in our own generation (Acts 13:36), it is important to realize that our God is very unlike the wicked judge or anyone else in our culture or sphere of influence. Noah did not have any God-honoring role models in his day while Lot did have the role model of Abraham. Their perspective of God came from their relationship with Him on a daily basis. It is in that daily relationship with our Friend, Jesus Christ, that faith is devel-

oped and nurtured. It is true that Noah's faith was greater in that he responded quietly and obediently to the revelations that God provided him. Lot, on the other hand, had weak faith and had to be forcibly dragged out of Sodom and Gomorrah with damaging consequences to him and his family. The wickedness that permeated the world at the time of Noah or that permeated the cities of Sodom and Gomorrah will also increase in our time. When the Son of Man returns, will He find saints pleasing in His sight? Will we be some of those saints?

6. For faith to blossom one must realize that there is a battle going on, and we have an adversary. Our adversary isn't just a wicked judge, but rather Satan, the world and the flesh. Sometimes, the adversarial nature of it all is very frontal and vicious: "Your adversary, the devil, prowls around like a roaring lion, seeking someone to devour. But resist him, firm in your faith" (1 Peter 5:8–9). Yet at other times, it can also be very subtle and vicious as well: "For even Satan disguises himself as an angel of light" (2 Corinthians 11:14). The goal of our adversary is to destroy our faith. Do we study the methods of the adversary so that we can recognize them? Or do we focus on knowing the Father, the Son and the Holy Spirit better? To focus on the ways of the enemy is to become more absorbed in him. And surely his attacks are cloaked in different

ways that it is impossible to discern unless one is in close fellowship with the Father. Thus, to spend the quality time with Jesus Christ and His Word, and to be obedient to that which He reveals, is the preferable way to guard our faith.

7. There are some unique similarities between the widow and believers today. First, this widow was truly alone just as God's elect are "widowed" today in Jesus' physical absence. However, while Jesus is not physically here, the spirit of Jesus Christ is still with us in the Holy Spirit so our "widowhood" is not as great. Second, the widow had a legitimate need just as God's people also have legitimate needs. The needs of people have not diminished with time! Third, the widow was weak as God's children are weak. Many of God's people today shun weakness, but our faith is undermined by not acknowledging our weakness, for Jesus said, "power is perfected in weakness" (2 Corinthians 12:9). As believers, we try to display or put forth strength or boast about our education, wealth, influence, manipulation or anything but weakness. God does not get the glory when the dependence is not on Him, and our faith does not progress but deteriorates when weakness is not an accepted reality of the saint. Fourth, the widow had no advocate, but we the saints today have an Advocate on high (Job 16:19). However, our Advocate doesn't just come to our aid

when tempted or in need of help (Hebrews 2:16, 18). He always lives to make intercession (Hebrews 7:25), but also His advocacy covers our sinning. 1 John 2:1 says, "If anyone sins [or is in the act of sinning], we have an Advocate with the Father, Jesus Christ the righteous."

The thoughts about the advocacy of Christ covering our sin and its impacts are profound. All of this affects the faith of a believer; for if a believer sins and does not confess the sin, his faith is undermined. We are commanded to confess our sins (1 John 1:9). When we do confess, "He is faithful and righteous to forgive us our sins and to cleanse us from all unrighteousness." Obedience to this command is an act of faith. In addition, it takes faith to believe God's Word that Jesus Christ is in the position of advocacy, and with this position He desires and prays for our best. Remember how Jesus knew that Peter would deny Him and thus prayed for his faith not to fail and for him to strengthen the saints when his faith was restored (Luke 22:31–32). This was an example of Jesus Christ in His role of Advocate for the betterment of Peter and others.

We need to walk in the power of the Holy Spirit daily and confess our sin as soon as we can when convicted by that same Spirit. That kind of moment-by-moment dependence cultivates the life of faith, encourages communication with the Father, enlarges the power of prayer and enables us to be part of what God wants to do in our lives and through us for others. Without this daily faith walk, there will indeed be few walking by faith when the Son of Man returns.

Questions for Reflection

1. The key question is, Will Jesus find faith on the earth when He returns? Will individuals be walking by faith, and will families be graciously living by faith? Will churches or ministries be nurturing the faith walk? What must you do from this point on to propagate living by faith?

2. "At all times they ought to pray" (Luke 18:1) is the exhortation from Jesus. In the last twenty-four hours, can you delineate the times that you prayed and what you prayed about? Make a list of the times and what you prayed about it. Lay the list before the Lord and ask Him to adjust your prayer life!

3. Is your praying in a rut? Do you pray about the same things every day, or do you pray about different things each day? How would keeping a prayer diary sharpen your prayer life? How does praying with others from time to time enrich your prayer life?

4. Have you ever persevered in prayer for something or someone for a long time? What did you learn about God from the experience? What did you learn about yourself?

5. Do you remember some circumstances that you passed through where you began to or did lose heart? How did God meet and sustain you in these circumstances? Share God's faithfulness with someone else who likewise may be losing heart.

6. When God sovereignly places you in a position of complete helplessness, what feelings and thoughts do you have about yourself and God? What tensions do you sense in this position of helplessness? What is the nature of your prayer life in these times?

Chapter 11

Have Faith in God

Read Matthew 21:18–22 and Mark 11:12–14, 19–26

We tend to have faith in our upbringing, education, experience, whom we know, how much money or resources we have, past successes, natural or spiritual gifts, ourselves, institutions or anything but our God. These kinds of dependencies blind us and make us unwilling to be in a position where God is all that we have and want. The disciples were in the same position! Jesus was now in Jerusalem for His last Passover (Mark 11:1), and in less than a week He would be crucified. He seemed to be running out of time to instruct and to develop the disciples in their faith in Him and God's Word. For sure, some drastic steps were needed to illustrate walking by faith and to provide impetus to His words to the disciples so that they could recall them later.

As a result, in the 21st chapter of Matthew (verses 20–22) and the 11th chapter of Mark (verses 20–26), Jesus performs a unique miracle to provide a springboard for teaching about faith in God and to leave an unforgettable mark on the hearts and minds of the disciples. Later recollection of this event and Jesus' words would be a tremendous boost to their faith in God.

Circumstance for Teaching

Jesus in His omniscience knew that eleven of His disciples had placed faith in Him and that one would betray Him. He had also observed over the past two years His disciples' weak faith, little faith and no faith (as noted in earlier chapters). There had been little progression in the life of faith for His closest followers. Some might say that was to be expected in the absence of the Holy Spirit and could not be rectified until the Holy Spirit was sent in Acts (chapter 1). On the other hand, when believers today exhibit the same patterns of weak faith, little faith and no faith even with the abiding presence of the Holy Spirit, what is our excuse?

To capture the attention of the disciples and to provide a providential circumstance for teaching them about faith, Jesus performs a destructive miracle on a fig tree. This is the only direct destructive miracle Jesus performed in His ministry (although indirectly there was destruction of the pigs in Mark 5:13 after casting the legion of demons out of the Gerasene demoniac). For sure, this fig tree miracle would test the disciples' observational powers, and depending upon their response, it provides Him an opportunity to talk about faith. The synthesis of Mark 11:12–15, 19–22 and Matthew 21:18–20 follows:

> [2]On the next day ([1]in the morning), when they had left Bethany ([1]returning to the city) He became hungry. [1]Seeing [2]at a distance [1]a lone fig tree by the road [2]in leaf, He went to see if perhaps He would find anything on it; and when He came to it, He found nothing but leaves, for it was not the season for figs. He said to it {the tree}, [1]"No longer shall there ever be any fruit from you." [2]"May no one ever eat fruit from you again!" And His disciples were listening. [1]And at once the fig tree withered. [2]Then they came to Jerusalem...When evening came, they would go out of the city.

> [2]As they were passing by in the morning, they saw the fig tree withered from the roots up. [1]The disciples were amazed and asked, "How did the fig tree wither all at once?" [2]Being reminded, Peter said to Him, "Rabbi, look, the fig tree which You cursed has withered." And Jesus answered saying to them, "Have faith in God."

It is evident that because Jesus was hungry, He sought fruit on a fig tree. The fig tree produces leaves in March or April and bears fruit two or even three times during a year: June, August and sometimes even in December. The presence of leaves could have indicated the presence of fruit, but there was none. As a result, Jesus curses the tree and says that it will never again bear fruit for anyone to eat. What Jesus said to the fig tree, the disciples heard. The next morning the disciples noticed that the fig tree had completely withered up. They recognized this as unusual since the normal withering process of trees takes time, but they connected the withering with the previous day's cursing of the tree by Jesus.

Jesus' curse of the fig tree and the recognition of the withered tree by the disciples were all part of the divine plan to be able to instruct the disciples on the topic of faith. Certainly there is a lesson here also on the failure of Israel to be fruitful for God in light of the divine privileges and benefits bestowed on them but even more so in light of the divine visitation of God's Son. More importantly, however, was the critical lesson on faith for the current and future disciples.

The track record of the disciples, according to the Gospels, was little faith, weak faith and no faith. This unique circumstance showed that there was some faith even though little or very weak. How do we reach that conclusion? If the disciples had said nothing or observed nothing about the fig tree in light of the Savior's words, that would have indicated hardened or insensitive hearts. Quite the contrary, the disciples do comment on the withered fig tree, and this indicates that some faith was there.

First, there was the spoken Word of God to the fig tree. The tree probably began to wither at Jesus' words, but the disciples did not notice the withered fig tree until the next morning. Second, there was a lag between the spoken Word of God and the reality of the words regarding the actual withered fig tree from the disciples' perspective. The salient point is that God tests our faith today by what we hear of the Word of God and how we apply it to circumstances later. If believers today want to please the Father in heaven, they will surely experience such divinely lagged circumstances or lagged perception of such circumstances as the disciples did.

Command to Have Faith

In light of the disciples' recognition of the withered fig tree, Jesus answers them with a command, "Have faith in God." He did not say they should have faith in themselves, in their abilities, in their resources, in programs, in the Jewish establishment of their day, in government, in their upbringing, in their education or lack of education or in anything else. He said to have faith in God. For over two plus years, Jesus observed their faith in action as weak, little or none at all. The lack of progress in the realm of faith by the disciples was surely disturbing to Jesus in light of His departure. Their weak faith is assuredly the reason why God sent Moses and Elijah to Jesus on the Mount of Transfiguration to speak with Him "of His departure which He was about to accomplish at Jerusalem" (Luke 9:30-31). Jesus had already told the disciples at least once very plainly that the "Son of Man must suffer many things and be rejected by the elders and the chief priests and the scribes, and be killed, and after three days rise again" (Mark 8:31–32). However, His followers did not receive these truths very well (Mark 8:32–38). Instead, they were caught up in the thinking and teaching of their day, that when the Messiah came He would establish and activate His kingdom—political and spiritual—on earth. They did not see or understand that the Messiah's first coming would be to fulfill the role of the "Lamb of God" to take away the sin of the world. Their preconceived ideas of what was to happen undermined their faith and did not allow them to understand the truths from the mouth of their Savior. As a result of not being able to provide any encouragement to their Savior, God provided divine encouragement from two who had departed earth previously. The disciples' weak faith and lack of understanding of the events to unfold as predicted by Jesus cause even the Father in heaven to gently admonish them in His words, "This is My Son, My Chosen One; listen to Him!" (Luke 9:35).

Two later exposures (Mark 9:31–32 and Mark 10:33–34) to the same truths about His death and resurrection, plus some additional insights, did not unite with faith either. In light of that response, Jesus attempts a last formal teaching on faith, which the disciples could recall later in the event their faith was still so small. He does this by using the situation of the withered fig tree. The verb in this context is present tense; and since it is an imperative verb, it is a command for these disciples (and us too) to have faith in God. The present tense here implies that a disciple of our Lord is to have faith in Him in a continuous way: not just once a week, not just occasionally, not just a small part of a day, but continuously day in and day out, in all spheres of life. Living by faith is to be a continuous process for every believer for "without faith it is impossible to please Him" (Hebrews 11:6). But that same believer needs to be mindful that sin destroys our walk of faith unless we confess it and keep short accounts with our Father in heaven (1 John 1:9).

We cannot escape these words, "Have faith in God." Jesus spoke them to the disciples, and they speak to us today. Many today say that they have faith, but there is no outward evidence of that faith. Consider the words of James:

> What use is it, my brethren, if someone says he has faith but he has no works? Can that faith save him? If a brother or sister is without clothing and in need of daily food, and one of you says to them, "Go in peace, be warmed and be filled," and yet you do not give them what is necessary for their body, what use is that? Even so faith, if it has no works, is dead, being by itself. But someone may well say, "You have faith and I have works; show me your faith without the works, and I will show you my faith by my works." (James 2:14–18)

Faith that is alive and dynamic produces good works. Paul writes in his letter to the Ephesians, "For we are His workmanship, created in Christ Jesus for good works, which God prepared beforehand so that we would walk in them" (2:10). How do we walk in them? By faith in God and nothing else!

Condition One and Faith in God

Immediately after Jesus' command to "have faith in God," there are two conditional statements from his lips as synthesized from the Matthew 21:21–22 and Mark 11:22–26 accounts:

> [2]Have faith in God. [1]Truly I say to you, if you have faith and do not doubt, you will not only do what was done to the fig tree, but even if you say to this mountain, "Be taken up and cast into the sea," [2]and does not doubt in his heart but believes that what he says is going to happen, it will be granted him. Therefore I say to you, [1]all things you ask in prayer [2]believe that you have received them, and they will be granted you. Whenever you stand praying, forgive, if you have anything against anyone, so that your Father who is in heaven will also forgive you your transgressions. [But if you do not forgive, neither will your Father who is in heaven forgive your transgressions.]

In the original Greek language, the statement reads, "If you have faith and do not doubt." This reflects a condition that is generally true in the present or probably realizable in the future for Christians. The track record of the disciples' weak faith over the past two years of Jesus' ministry indicates that their faith was not at a mature level currently for they were not seizing on all of His words. Instead, they were picking and choosing what they wanted to believe. For example, they believed that Jesus was the Son of God, the Messiah. However, they did not believe or understand that He must die first and then be resurrected even though He had stated the matter plainly in Mark 8:31–32.

In addition, prior to this discussion on faith, Jesus had performed three resurrections in His ministry when He raised Jairus' daughter (Mark 5: 35–43, a resurrection that occurred in a complete family), when He raised a widow's son (Luke 7:11–16, a resurrection for a single-parent family) and when He raised Lazarus, the brother of Mary and Martha (John 11, a resurrection for a no-parent family). In the first two resurrections, the time of death was less than a day, while in the case of Lazarus four to five days had transpired. Thus, there was much evidence to the truth of the resurrection as attested to by Deuteronomy 19:15, which says, "On the evidence of two or three witnesses a matter shall be confirmed." It should not have been difficult to believe that the Son of Man could also be raised. While these things did not connect with faith in the hearts of the disciples, Jesus believed that one day their unwavering trust in God and His Word would be there. In that day, there would be no doubt in their hearts for doubt and faith in God cannot co-exist in the same heart.

If we have faith and do not doubt, we will be able to do not only what was done to the fig tree, but we will be able to do the impossible by saying to this mountain, "Be taken up and cast into the sea." Jesus just spoke the Word to the fig tree and it withered by the next morning. Today, we may see many such withered-fig-tree-type miracles, but they have not been done by faith but by the flesh. Remember that God told Moses to speak to the rock (the second time) in Numbers 20, but Moses in his rashness struck the rock with his rod. Water came forth abundantly, even in light of Moses' disobedi-ence because the need of the people and animals for water was greater than dealing with Moses at that very moment. This is a withered-fig-tree-type miracle that was performed in the flesh, but God held Moses accountable for not treating Him as holy in the sight of the congregation of Israel by not allowing him to go into the Promised Land. Like-wise, today it is possible with certain chemicals to make fig trees wither and die within hours. How-ever, to move mountains—the impossible—it will take faith.

With that being said, the believer today must refrain from fleshing out solutions to situations that he could flesh out. Not trusting God in such circumstances undermines our faith to be able to move mountains. When God delays answering in a situation that we have prayed about, our faith in Him is undermined greatly when we display doubt with our fleshly solutions. Just to pray about a situation is no guarantee that we will have what we ask. Our request must be based on the Word of God, nestled completely in the character of God and prompted by the Holy Spirit. That is the essence of faith! However, that kind of faith may need to keep asking and not doubting for days, weeks, months or years. Hebrews 10:36 says it well: "For you have need of endurance, so that when you have done the will of God, you may receive what was promised." The timelines for endurance, praying and not doubting are varied to expand and mold our faith in our sovereign God. That is as it should be if we are to grow in faith!

Finally, Jesus knew that His disciples and future disciples would face many impossible situations, which He expressed as mountains that needed moving. The mountains will take various forms. They could be in the form of the unexpected death of a child, being told that you or a loved one has cancer, having a family member with a serious drug or alcohol addiction, being laid off of a job, being sandwiched between caring for your children and your elderly parents and countless other situations. There will be commonality between some of the mountains believers face in life and ministry, but there will also be strange things uniquely designed by God to enlarge our faith if we respond rightly (1 Peter 4:12–13). In them all, one must "have faith in God" and God alone!

Condition Two and Forgiveness

The second conditional statement occurs in Mark 11:25–26 in the context of praying. This condition occurs after the statement "whenever you stand praying" as noted: "Whenever you stand praying, forgive, if you have anything against anyone, so that your Father who is in heaven will also forgive you your transgressions. [But if you do not forgive, neither will your Father who is in heaven forgive your transgressions.]"

The Apostle Paul said believers should pray without ceasing (1 Thessalonians 5:17) or at all times in the Spirit (Ephesians 6:18). In addition, we should also monitor the way we approach God with our petitions. Frequently, we do not have because we do not ask, or we ask and do not receive because we ask with wrong motives (James 4:2–3). Is it possible that we do not ask because we believe that we can flesh out our own solution or that it is too unimportant to bother God about? Is it possible that we rationalize nonanswers from God as being outside His will rather than seeing that our asking was not with godly motives? Is it possible that we had not forgiven someone else for a wrong or perceived wrong?

The second condition for having faith in God is expressed in the statement, "If you have anything against anyone. . . ." The structure of this conditional proposition is an assumed reality, either now or later. That is, we all will have trouble with forgiveness, either toward someone else who has actually or seemingly wronged us or even toward ourselves. Even so, the lack of forgiveness toward that individual or individuals (or even ourselves) will undermine our prayer and our faith in God. "If we confess our sins, He is faithful and righteous to forgive us our sins and to cleanse us from all unrighteousness" (1 John 1:9). Believers need to keep short accounts with God by confessing their sin or their lack of forgiveness toward another as quickly as possible. The failure to do so could lead to bitterness and defilement not only of the individual saint but also of many others (Hebrews 12:15).

In summary, the lack of a forgiving spirit toward others means that we do not appreciate or fully understand how God in Christ also has forgiven us (Ephesians 4:32). Second, the lack of forgiveness undermines our prayer lives in that we may not feel the need for prayer since we want to nurse our grudge or ill feelings toward another. Either that or we pray with many words but no power. Third, the failure to forgive another truly undermines our faith in God, His Word and His ways. The result is that we cannot see as He sees and pray as He wills. The net outcome of this nonappreciation of our forgiveness in Christ, our poor and impotent prayer life and our weakened faith in God is the lack of divine results and impacts that last forever. Life is not fair, and there are injustices that are humanly hard to forgive; but we must believe that a sovereign God has allowed them to perfect our faith in Him so that we will be able to move mountains.

Life Response to Biblical Truth

1. What is obvious about this fig tree incident is that our God knows the stage of our faith, whether weak, little or almost none; and He desires us to progress and not stagnate or decline in faith. God is sovereign and sees and understands our failures in the realm of faith throughout the timeline of our spiritual life. But He is ever working, arranging events, or cornering us in such a way that we will have opportunities to respond by faith and thus begin or begin anew the great adventure of trust in Him and His Word. Some of these events or situations will be obvious opportunities for faith to blossom or deteriorate while others may be far from obvious in areas where we may have preconceived ideas that God has no interest. Such incorrect compartmental thinking sees God with an interest only in the macros of life and not the micros. God desires us to please Him in all that we do or think, and that requires faith. "For without faith it is impossible to please Him."

2. Believers are commanded to "have faith in God." This is a command not to take lightly,

and having faith in God should permeate our spiritual life, not just occasionally in big events but every week, every day and every hour of our life. Some might say that it is hard to know whether or not a believer has been obedient to this command. There can be behavior or deeds, such as Moses striking the rock the second time, that produce needed results—but not in the divine way. Or, as noted by Jesus in Matthew 23:28, "So you, too, outwardly appear righteous to men, but inwardly you are full of hypocrisy and lawlessness." Outward appearances can be very deceiving. The solution to this dilemma was modeled by Jesus Christ as He spent time with His disciples in many diverse situations, bringing the Word of God to the forefront for almost three years. Only in this way can true character be assessed. There is no large-scale way to shepherd and present believers complete in Christ (Colossians 1:28). It must be done in a small-group environment where the sheep can be known intimately and co-shepherded with the Chief Shepherd.

3. Which is the greatest miracle: withering fig trees or moving mountains? I confess that I cannot cause a fig tree to wither by my words as Jesus did, but I could take fleshy steps to get the fig tree to wither by applying some sort of chemical or poison that would kill the tree. Outwardly, the results would seem to be the same.

I could even go so far as to say the words, "No longer shall there ever be any fruit from you," and come back and apply the poison. The truth is that I would have been deceptive and not pleased God. Likewise, individual saints and Christian institutions have adopted the model (frequently the business model) to do all that they can (which is a lot) from a human point of view and only rely on God when there is no other way to flesh out a solution. Frequently, the manipulations and fleshly methods become so sophisticated and complex that it appears God did it, but God Himself knows otherwise. If He is not the Author and Perfecter of the solution, then we are not treating God as holy just as Moses did not treat Him as holy in striking the rock the second time. There will be dire consequences for us as there were for Moses; but more importantly our faith in God, His ways and His Word will be seriously undermined or compromised.

4. Certainly, the greatest miracle is to move mountains since it is going to require faith in a great God. Aside from blasting, there is no way humanly to move a mountain although many try. Small portions of the mountain could be moved and dumped into the sea, but Jesus had no such thought in mind. He said that one could "say to this mountain, 'Be taken up and cast into the sea.'" That is an impossible situation without

divine intervention. We must understand that the sovereign God places mountains before us in order for us to exercise faith in Him. The end result is that He is pleased and our faith grows; and at a later time, He will place a bigger mountain before us that also can only be moved by faith. The right biblical response in each situation will be a faith in God that is entrenched in His Word and His character.

5. Jesus' words to the disciples, "everything you shall ask in prayer," as well as the words of God through the Apostle Paul to "pray without ceasing" and to "pray at all times in the Spirit," all indicate that prayer should be as natural to the believer as breathing. For those prayers to be effective, they must be grounded in faith in God and His Word, and they must also be grounded in constant communion with the Father. This kind of divine communication is short-circuited by the overuse of technology available to Christians today: cell phones, iPods, computers and more. How can one listen to God and know how to pray and to exercise faith when there is no stillness to hear God and to study His Word? We tend to want to schedule God in our busy or multitasking lives, but our Lord cannot be confined to a scheduled time. Rather, He desires and demands to be the Author and Perfecter of all we do and are, and He wants us to put our faith in His time frame.

6. "When you stand praying, forgive" were the words of Jesus here in the 11th chapter of Mark. Failing to show forgiveness to another is sin, and that sin undermines our prayers and our faith. When that happens, our spiritual senses cease to function properly. As Tozer has written, "Where faith is defective the result will be inward insensibility and numbness toward spiritual things."[1] For instance, in my dealings and interactions with others, I frequently hear arrogant or exaggerated statements that could be harmful to not only me but others. Under the conviction of the Holy Spirit, I must move to forgive them, or my prayers and faith will be contaminated. With a few moments of reflection, I too remember that I have likewise been guilty of such sin, but God in Christ has forgiven me. I, in turn, must forgive or risk failure in the life of faith and true fellowship with the Father. A true believer will not give up these two realities.

Questions for Reflection

1. To continually have faith in God is the admonition from Scripture. Make a list of the things that you have trusted in instead of God (read Jeremiah 11:13). How can one be sure that he is trusting in God and not these other things?

2. How can one tell if he or she has fleshed out the cursing of a fig tree situation instead of doing it by faith? Why are moving-mountain experiences critical in the life of faith? Reflect on these issues or discuss with another.

3. Weak faith is seriously undermined by poor application or no application of truth. How do you apply biblical truth that you hear? Why is the daily application of Scriptures necessary to walking by faith?

4. Our faith can also be strongly weakened by not being able to forgive others. How does one work through an injustice, mistreatment, slander or backstabbing situation where you may find it almost impossible to forgive?

5. Do you have close relationships with other believers who would exhort you to have faith in a great God? How do you cultivate such relationships? What is the value of such relationships for those of us who want to walk by faith in all we do?

6. The aftermath of the cursing of the fig tree was a teachable divine moment. How do we learn to recognize such teachable moments? What must our perspective of God be to see these teachable moments rightly?

Chapter 12

Faith That Fails;
Faith That Strengthens

Read Matthew 26:30–46; Mark 14:26–42;
Luke 22:31–34, 39–46

The last explicit discussion about faith was between Jesus and Peter, and it is recorded in the
22nd chapter of the Gospel of Luke:

> "Simon, Simon, behold, Satan has demanded permission
> to sift you like wheat; but I have prayed for you, that
> your faith may not fail; and you, when once you have
> turned again, strengthen your brothers." But he said to
> Him, "Lord, with You I am ready to go both to prison
> and to death!" And He said, "I say to you, Peter, the
> rooster will not crow today until you have denied three
> times that you know Me." (Luke 22:31–34)

It is difficult to tell whether this discussion occurred in the upper room or after the Upper Room Discourse (John 13–17). If it was in the upper room, this discussion came right after the following words from Jesus' lips:

> "Little children, I am with you a little while longer. You will seek Me; and as I said to the Jews, now I also say to you, 'Where I am going, you cannot come.' A new commandment I give to you, that you love one another, even as I have loved you, that you also love one another. By this all men will know that you are My disciples, if you have love for one another." Simon Peter said to Him, "Lord, where are You going?" Jesus answered, "Where I go, you cannot follow Me now; but you will follow later." Peter said to Him, "Lord, why can I not follow You right now? I will lay down my life for You." Jesus answered, "Will you lay down your life for Me? Truly, truly, I say to you, a rooster will not crow until you deny Me three times." (John 13:33–38)

If this is the precursory event in the upper room to Jesus' words about faith in the passage in Luke, then there is an extreme significance to be attached to this new commandment to love one another. This was to be the mark of a true disciple of Jesus Christ. One could easily make a case that this dovetails well with Jesus' restoration of Peter in John 21:15–23 when He asks Peter three times if he loved Him.

On the other hand, if this discussion on faith is after the Upper Room Discourse, then Matthew 26:30–35 might indicate the timeline.

After singing a hymn, they went out to the Mount of Olives. Then Jesus said to them, "You will all fall away because of Me this night, for it is written, 'I WILL STRIKE DOWN THE SHEPHERD, AND THE SHEEP OF THE FLOCK SHALL BE SCATTERED.' But after I have been raised, I will go ahead of you to Galilee." But Peter said to Him, "Even though all may fall away because of You, I will never fall away." Jesus said to him, "Truly I say to you that this very night, before a rooster crows, you will deny Me three times." Peter said to Him, "Even if I have to die with You, I will not deny You." All the disciples said the same thing too.

In this case, Jesus educates the disciples on the reality from Scripture that the Shepherd would be struck down and the sheep scattered. If God said it, there is no denying that what the Scriptures predict is going to happen. In addition, Jesus reminds the disciples for at least the fourth time (Mark 8:31, 9:31–32, 10:33–34) that He would be raised from the dead. The new information from this discourse is that He would go into Galilee after the resurrection.

These last words about faith occur in Luke 22:31–34, but it is still difficult to tell if the conversation was in the upper room or afterward. However, the precursory event in that chapter of Luke is "a dispute among them as to which one of them was regarded to be greatest" (22:24). These kinds of discussions seemed to occur while the disciples were traveling with Jesus as indicated by the Gospel of Mark on another occasion: "They came to Capernaum; and when He was in the house, He began to question them, 'What were you discussing on the way?' But they kept silent, for on the way they had discussed with one another which of them was the greatest" (Mark 9:33–34).

The point to be made about this timeline is that it seems to have occurred after the upper room and after Jesus said the following on being a servant:

> And He said to them, "The kings of the Gentiles lord it over them; and those who have authority over them are called 'Benefactors.' But it is not this way with you, but the one who is the greatest among you must become like the youngest, and the leader like the servant. For who is greater, the one who reclines at the table or the one who serves? Is it not the one who reclines at the table? But I am among you as the one who serves." (Luke 22:25–27)

This correlates well with Jesus' words to Peter to strengthen or serve his brothers after he turns back again to the Lord. One could make a strong case that love for one another drives this kind of service as well, but the essence of Jesus' words seems to spring from Him wanting His disciples to be servants not kings.

Permission to Sift

The words of Jesus to Peter, "Simon, Simon, behold, Satan has demanded permission to sift you like wheat" (Luke 22:31) drip with truths that are very pertinent to our faith. First, the root verb here for "demanded permission" indicates a request from one in a lesser position to one in a higher position, as a child to a parent, a beggar to a passerby or as a man or woman to God. This is significant in that God is over all and that nothing can happen to us unless He allows it. As the Old Testament book of Job clearly teaches, God is in the seat of power and control, not Satan. Satan can only do what God allows Him to do. Second, the verb for demanded permission could be translated "asked or demanded for himself." It is critical to know that Satan never wants God's best for God's people. On the contrary, he wants the worst or whatever will drive them away from dependence upon God and His Word. The enemy's motive is always anti-God and anti-faith, but God uses all that Satan is and does to work out His best in our faith and lives. God is never surprised by these requests from the adversary. We must ever remember that God is omniscient, and Satan is not.

A third unique aspect of these words was that Satan wanted permission to sift "you." This "you" is plural, indicating that Satan wanted to sift all of the disciples, not just one. The scattering of all of the disciples like sheep would leave the Shepherd alone. In the book of Job, the testing of Job is of one, not many, although Job's family was affected as well.

A fourth aspect is the request to sift like wheat. When sifting or winnowing, one attempts to separate the wheat and the chaff by using the wind. God's design is to allow Satan in this situation to separate the wheat and chaff in their hearts, minds and spiritual understandings such that the end result would be a higher quality or purity of life and faith. Of course, Satan's design is to destroy the faith of the believer in any way possible.

What is truly significant about this request from Satan is that God did allow it! Why? Three reasons come to mind. One was to fulfill the prophecy of Zechariah 13:7: "Strike the Shepherd that the sheep may be scattered." The fulfillment of this prophecy is more than just proving true the Word of God; but it also provides testimony to those who would later believe on the realities of the death and resurrection of Jesus Christ. The second reason was to purify and mature the faith of the disciples. Without this sifting, their faith would not progress to where it needed to be in order to change the world. The third reason for this sifting was to inform and illustrate for future disciples that God does allow the bottom to drop out of our lives to gently force us to realize that He is in control, He will mature our faith and that what He is doing is for our best. God never wastes time and experiences even if Satan has been allowed to have a hand in these tests of faith.

Prayer of Another

Satan requested permission to sift the disciples, and that permission was granted. In almost the same breath, however, Jesus made it clear that He had already prayed for them. It may have been a surprise from the human side of the events, but there was no surprise about the sifting to come from the divine side. Jesus knew about it from the Scriptures (Zechariah 13:7), but He moves to His role as Intercessor "since He always lives to make intercession for them" (Hebrews 7:25). When going through a shocking sequence of events, such as loss of a job, a serious illness or death of a child, a child or relative caught in drug addiction, the death of a parent or an unexpected death of a friend or relative, it is encouraging to know that what has been allowed has passed through the hands of God and that God's Son is praying for us. We may be agonizing with the pains of the moment and the uncertainties of the future, but our Lord in His omnipresence and omniscience sees it all, knows what could and should be and prays for us.

The content of the Lord's prayer for us in these agonizing, difficult and impossible moments is threefold. First (and it is first), He prays that our faith may not fail. Our Lord knows that such heart-wrenching experiences could weaken our faith or lead us further from God instead of closer to Him. They could even cause us to deny Him. These are the results that Satan would like to accomplish, and he would love us to follow the foolish counsel of Job's wife, "Curse God and die;" (Job 2:9). Job recognized that the counsel of his wife was foolish and that the divine perspective of events was necessary: "Shall we indeed accept good from God and not accept adversity?" (Job 2:10). Our Lord knows our frailty in such faith-destructive events, He knows our helplessness in praying appropriately and He knows our inability to see as He sees.

Thankfully, the Master always lives to make intercession for us! And while our Lord prays for us, we are also commanded to pray for one another (James 5:16). We desperately need the prayers of other saints, for the battle we are engaged in is not against flesh and blood "but against the rulers, against the powers, against the world forces of this darkness, against the spiritual forces of wickedness in the heavenly places" (Ephesians 6:12). Jesus' disciples were in a unique position, for aside from Jesus, they had no one else to pray for them.

The second aspect of Jesus' prayer is that this failure or this detour is certain and that the return again of the "you" (or Peter in this case) to the Savior is also certain. Jesus not only prayed that the faith of the disciples would not fail, but He also knew in answer to that prayer that Peter would recover from this failure in faith. As believers, we all will experience failure or detours in the faith. They can be overwhelming and disqualifying, but our God desires that these momentary glitches in our lives purify us, enhance our faith and lead to the betterment of others. Again, the Lord is never surprised by these failures, but He desires that we press on in our relationship with Him despite it all. In the grand scheme of things, God uses the failures, detours and stumblings to accomplish not only great things in our lives but also to build our faith that is more precious than gold (1 Peter 1:7).

The third aspect of Jesus' prayer was for Peter to strengthen his brothers and sisters in Christ. When we fail, stumble, take a detour in the faith, all these things are His servants (Psalm 119:91) to make us weak and more dependent on Him. The Lord's power is perfected in our weakness (2 Corinthians 12:9), and it is in that weakness that we can minister more effectively to others. The same word for strengthen is also used in the first letter of Thessalonians (3:2) to describe Timothy's work among the Thessalonians to strengthen and encourage their faith. When we fail in our faith, we may not have all of the answers to avoid or prevent the failure of faith in others. However, we can communicate the divine process of restoration that God has accomplished in our lives so that the faith of others is strengthened and encouraged.

Personal Response

When confronted with truth about ourselves from whatever source (family, friends, enemies, Scriptures, pastor, mate or the Lord Himself), we are quick to deny the reality or the possibility of that truth pertaining to us. We do not like to receive admonitions or truth from any source that points out our weaknesses, our propensities and our sins. This is true not only for individuals but also churches and Christian organizations. We tend to be like the king in Ecclesiastes 4: "A poor yet wise lad is better than an old and foolish king who no longer knows how to receive instruction" (verse 13). This king once knew how to receive truth; but age or time, divinely appointed position, hardness of heart, lack of accountability and mind-set of being more like God than dependent on God destroyed this king's faith and his ability to receive truth or admonition. Though we will deny it, we are no different today for the Scriptures say that "the heart is more deceitful than all else and is desperately sick" (Jeremiah 17:9).

Individual believers, pastors and Christian leaders have all been confronted with truth or observations about our slippage away from the truth. Sorry to say, most of us ignore such admonition and retreat back into our core of friends or to those in our support group who have the same problem(s) we have or who don't have the courage to say anything to us under the inspiration of the Holy Spirit. The end result is that we discard the admonition as coming from a disgruntled, dissatisfied, disenchanted or disingenuous individual or individuals. Interestingly, Peter tries the same approach, but the truths being ignored and discounted were coming from the Son of God.

In typical form, prior to the cross, Peter responds quickly and rashly. He makes the following boast: "And he said to Him, 'Lord, with You I am ready to go, both to prison and death.'" In these words, "Lord, with You," there is something commendable but unhealthy. The commendable is the dependence perspective reflected in Jesus' words in John 15:5, "Apart from Me you can do nothing." We should always want to walk with Jesus in whatever we go through and to feel and know that His presence is with us. However, the unhealthy side of Peter's words is revealed in the words of Job and Isaiah as noted below:

> Behold, I go forward but He is not there, and backward, but I cannot perceive Him; when He acts on the left, I cannot behold Him; He turns on the right, I cannot see Him. But He knows the way I take; When He has tried me, I shall come forth as gold. . . . But I am not silenced by the darkness, nor deep gloom which covers me. (Job 23:8–10, 17)

> Oh that I were as in months gone by, as in the days when God watched over me; when His lamp shone over my head, and by His light I walked through darkness; as I was in the prime of my days, when the friendship of God was over my tent. (Job 29:2–4)

> Who is among you that fears the LORD, that obeys the voice of His servant, that walks in darkness and has no light? Let him trust in the name of the LORD and rely on his God. Behold, all you who kindle a fire, who encircle yourselves with firebrands, walk in the light of your fire and among the brands you have set ablaze. (Isaiah 50:10–11)

These passages communicate several key points. First, there are times when the presence of God can be felt, and at those times we feel like we can conquer the world. Yet our dependence could be upon the presence or the feeling of that presence of God and not actually on God and His Word. Second, as a result of this perception, God removes His presence or hides Himself so that our faith is in Him and His Word and not a feeling. He wants us to walk by faith, not by sight (2 Corinthians 5:7). That is why we have times where the Lord God cannot be perceived. Third, these times seem to be filled with darkness and not light. Whichever direction we turn—right or left, backwards or forward—the silence can be deafening, frightening and maybe even depressing. Fourth, these times are again allowed by God to test and build our faith. In fact, if accepted as from God's hand, such times can greatly enrich our faith because they drive us to the Scriptures as never before!

Peter said that he was ready to go with Jesus. But what believer willingly volunteers for such "enriching experiences" as Peter did? No saint is ever ready for what these experiences of God's distance or hiding will reveal about themselves, their faith or about God. Peter was going to go through a time without the closeness of Jesus, and he was going to fail miserably. What is encouraging is that Jesus knew that Peter would fail and prayed for him. If what was mentioned in Job and Isaiah as well as in Peter's situation is true (and it is), we are never ready for these "enriching experiences" where the closeness of God is distant, where darkness seems to have swallowed up light and where failure may be imminent.

Three principles come out of the prophets and Jesus' words to Peter. First, God must take us to these experiences of His deafening silence and His seeming absence in His way and His time. There is no way to volunteer or to accelerate our entry into them. Second, "Let him trust in the name of the Lord and rely on his God." When going through these times and experiences, our trust or our faith in God and His various names is the key to enduring. The names of God—El Shaddai, Jehovah-Jireh, Shepherd, Branch and many more—all have simplicity and a depth to them that sustains the soul that clings to God. The third principle is a warning against lighting our own fire. If surrounded with experiences of darkness and uncertainty, we need to be careful that we don't generate our own light by self-effort, manipulations of others or power games of the flesh. To do so will undermine our faith and keep us from learning what God intended for us. In this case, our faith does not mature. Jesus wanted Peter's faith to mature, not digress, and so He prayed for him.

Prophetic Reality

The Apostle Peter's confidence that he was ready to go with Jesus to prison and death was not in line with what Jesus foreknew. How does such false confidence get exposed? God uses failure to humble and break the individual so that he or she will be teachable and supple in His hands. Jesus loved Peter very much, but to prepare him to strengthen his fellow saints afterwards: (a) He predicted what Peter would do, (b) what He predicts comes true and (c) what He prays comes to pass. In this way, the reality of Deuteronomy 19:15 was to be affirmed: "On the evidence of two or three witnesses a matter shall be confirmed." This affirmation would not only work out for Peter's best but also for the best of the rest of the disciples and all other saints who follow and want to truly understand living by faith.

The prophetic reality of what Jesus said about Peter is probably best expressed in Matthew 26:34–35: "Jesus said to him, 'Truly I say to you that this very night, before a rooster crows, you will deny Me three times.' Peter said to Him, 'Even if I have to die with You, I will not deny You.' All the disciples said the same thing too."

Jesus knew better, and His reply was very specific: this very night, before a cock crows and three denials. All the Lord Jesus predicted came true, and the net result was that Peter "went out and wept bitterly" (Matthew 26:75). The answer to Jesus' prayer about the restoration of Peter and Peter strengthening his brothers does not move closer to completion until the 1st chapter of Acts. Three days later, the restoration process begins when Peter and John race to the empty tomb (John 20:2–10). The restoration of Peter continues with Jesus' special appearance to Peter (Luke 24:34, 1 Corinthians 15:5) and several post-resurrection appearances as well (John 20:19–23, 24–29, 21:1–24). In this last appearance after breakfast, Jesus asks three times if Peter loved Him. Peter answers in the affirmative each time, and Jesus responded with three commands: Tend My lambs, shepherd My sheep and lastly, tend My sheep. The matter of utmost importance was the strengthening of his brothers as Jesus had prayed for Peter. That reality would begin in Acts 1.

The last aspect of Peter's restoration is reflected in Jesus' command to Peter to "follow Me!" (John 21:19). Before the crucifixion of Christ, Peter exuded confidence in the flesh, claiming he would follow Jesus to prison and death. The reality was that he was not ready! In the flesh, there is no power for the tasks in life and ministry, apart from a moment-by-moment dependence upon God in the power of the Holy Spirit. That empowerment for Peter was going to come (Acts 1), but he needed to know that the initiative in following Jesus was not his. It is God's word to Peter and us today to follow Him in the power of the Holy Spirit. Nothing has changed!

Life Response to Biblical Truth

1. All believers will fail, stumble or experience detours in the faith as a result of the world, the flesh or the devil himself. Sometimes, these fi-

ery ordeals, which come upon us for our testing, will seem strange, and from the divine side they are indeed strange (1 Peter 4:12). However, as in Peter's case, these difficult circumstances are allowed by God to test our hearts, minds and faith. If Satan is involved, he has been given permission to be involved; and he uses that permission to destroy our faith. But God desires to use the "enriching experiences" to mold, purify and enrich our faith for our own personal spiritual gain and as a testimony to nonbelievers and believers alike. In addition, God uses these experiences to strengthen the faith and walk of other saints.

2. While we may be surprised by the loss of a job, the sudden death of a loved one or some other tragic situation, God is never surprised! From the beginning of time, the Creator and Redeemer has always known what would happen. Could He have avoided the situation? Yes! Could He have produced a different outcome? Yes! However, in His omniscience and omnipotence, He also knew where our faith and relationship with Him would be. He also knew who might be currently watching our response or who would be ministered to later with the outworking of His design for us to be more like Him. God, the infinite One, sees it all since He is not constrained by time, and He understands that what He does in our life impacts not only us but many others.

Jesus was not surprised by the denials that were to come from Peter, but the Messiah was going to use them all for good (Romans 8:28).

3. No matter what form these trials (failure, stumblings, detours, denials or whatever) take, they can be overwhelming and disqualifying. Yet, we know with confidence that our Lord is ever praying for us that our faith may not fail but rather excel still more. In addition, He prayed for Peter that when he turned back again that he would strengthen his brothers. Jesus' prayer was for the faith of Peter to not fail and the faith of others to be strengthened. Do we pray likewise?

    As I evaluate my prayer life, I find my focus too much on earthly things and not enough on the faith of others. Without closeness to people, we cannot know how to pray for their faith as Jesus did for Peter. This may explain our lack of power in praying in that we are not praying as Jesus would. We are not omniscient, and so we need to be cultivating close relationships with others inside and outside the body of Christ.

4. When confronted with unpleasant truth about ourselves or our ministry, we usually respond just like Peter did. We deny it! We first rationalize our denial by dismissing the source of the criticism or confrontation. If God had spoken from the heavens, we might listen; but our hardness

of heart would explain that away too by saying it just thundered (John 12:29). If the admonition came from a friend, it would probably come sugarcoated since it is flavored with sympathy. If it comes from an enemy or critic, then the admonition comes with greater sting or frankness.

The second rationalization for denying admonition is the tone that is used. An older Christian once graciously remarked to me that when receiving admonition or criticism, pay little attention to the tone and harshness of the words—just pay attention to the truth. Peter could not ignore the source, the tone or the words of the Author and Perfecter of his faith. We too cannot afford to miss the admonition coming as a gentle breeze or else we may be forced to hear it in tornados, earthquakes or fires of life (1 Kings 19:9–14). The latter is not the best option for our faith to mature since it will require more drastic actions and more personal pain from God to get our attention.

5. All the disciples went through during their two plus years with Jesus was meant to perfect their faith. There were some small successes, but mostly there were failures. Maybe they had become accustomed to the miraculous events and the presence of Jesus. In Judges 2:10, it is recorded that "there arose another generation after them who did not know the LORD, nor yet

the work which He had done for Israel." When Joshua, the elders and the rest of his generation died, the concepts of faith and obedience to the Word of God had not been passed on to the next generation. Jesus wanted the faith of Peter and all of the disciples to blossom and to be passed on, and that is why He prayed for them prior to the resurrection and continually afterwards. It is very significant that Jesus restored Peter with a special appearance (Luke 24:34, 1 Corinthians 15:5) and several post-resurrection appearances (John 20:19–23, 24–29, 21:1–24). This restoration took time and personal attention from the Lord. Likewise, today we are admonished to restore with a spirit of gentleness one caught in any trespass (Galatians 6:1). It will take time and energy, but it yields a fruit that bears more fruit!

6. I would expect that 99.9% of believers today would not make the boast that Peter made that "with You I am ready to go to prison and death." We should be able to do that if God calls us to it, but it is not a boast that we can make. However, we make boasts in other ways. For instance, "I'm going to be a good parent," and then one of our children gets into drugs or trouble with the law. Or, "I'm going to be faithful in tithing," and we lose our job and means to give. One can be sure that if we boast or exude self-confidence that "such and such is what I'm going to do," God in His infinite love for us will expose that

false boast and strip us of that self-confidence. He does that to build our dependence on Him, to decrease our dependence on ourselves and to protect His glory that He shares with no one.

7. Finally, many of our boasts of self-confidence come from a position of where God has given us much, where God's blessings have been truly evident or where the presence of God has been strongly felt in much that we do. In such circumstances, our faith may be in the blessings and not the One who blesses. This is a distorted faith, and our Father in heaven must act in such a way that faith is in Him and His Word and not the blessings. As noted in Job 23, Job 29 and Isaiah 50, God may hide Himself or withdraw His presence for a time to perfect our faith in Him. Be certain that He is not surprised by our boast. In the divine plan from eternity past, He has made accommodations for our boast of self-confidence in such a way that it is changed to a boast in the Lord only. That is the way of faith!

Questions for Reflection

1. God allows tough times, failure, sifting experiences, fiery ordeals and the like to prove our faith more precious than gold or silver. What have you learned about God in such past "enriching experiences"? What did you learn about yourself? In the current "enriching experience," what did you learn in the past that has enabled you to persevere in the present situation?

2. Satan for sure wants to destroy our faith, but our Lord ever intercedes for the saints that their faith may not fail and that they may strengthen others in Christ as a result of this "enriching experience." How does the intercession of the Lord on your behalf impact you during these tough times? What does that imply about our praying and others praying for us while going through these "enriching" experiences?

3. In your walk with Christ, have you ever experienced a time of darkness or the absence of light, a time of silence from the heavens, a perception of His presence not being there or all three? What did you learn about God in that "enriching experience"? What would you say to others about surviving and pressing on from such strange ordeals?

4. Almost all saints are surprised by the strange, fiery ordeals or "enriching experiences" that come their way, but God is never surprised. What comfort or encouragement comes from this reality?

5. How does one tell if they have been trusting in the blessings of God instead of the Blessed One Himself? Make a list of the names of God in both the Old and New Testament. What is the enriching value of meditating on these names in tough times?

6. Frequently, in our impatience with God and His ways during these "enriching experiences," we light our own fire or try to get out of it our way. What are the dangers of this approach for deliverance?

Chapter 13

Queries about Our Faith

Tozer had some very deep things to say about faith, and he has been quoted frequently in this book. His comments and implications about faith have been sprinkled throughout everything he wrote, but there is a concentration on the topic in several books, chapters or sermons. In his book *The Root of the Righteous*, in a chapter entitled, "Faith is a Perturbing Thing," Tozer said the following:

> Something has happened to the doctrine of justification by faith as Luther taught it. . . . The faith of Paul and Luther was a revolutionizing thing. It upset the whole life of the individual and made him into another person altogether. It laid hold on the life and brought it under obedience to Christ. It took up its cross and followed along after Jesus with no intention of going back. . . .

It made him little and God big and Christ unspeakably dear. All this and more happened to a man when he received the faith that justifies. . . . Little by little the whole meaning of the word shifted from what it had been to what it is now. . . . Faith now means no more than passive moral acquiescence in the Word of God and the cross of Jesus. To exercise it we have only to rest on one knee and nod our heads in agreement. . . . Such a faith as this does not perturb people. It comforts them. . . . This generation of Christians must hear again the doctrine of the perturbing quality of faith. . . . The only man who can be sure that he has true Bible faith is the one who has put himself in a position where he cannot go back.[1]

The person of faith puts himself or herself in a position of dependence upon God. Resting in that position, he or she can wait on God alone to lead, to protect and to deliver in His way and in His time.

With that said, this chapter on faith is an attempt to pull together the patterns and principles on walking by faith that are communicated in chapters 1 through 7, basically stages one and two of "children" and "young men" in the faith, respectively. All true believers will have to wrestle with food, clothing, shelter and the storms of life. These situations are arranged by God, and how believers respond will determine how their faith progresses or digresses. However, it also needs to be said that Christian institutions—whether churches or ministries—also have to wrestle with the same situations, and their responses will indicate whether they will be a faith-propagating entity or an anti-faith entity, favoring fleshly or businesslike practices that destroy living by faith.

Where Is Your Faith?

"Where is your faith?" is a question that Jesus asked the disciples after delivering them from the storm as recorded in the 8th chapter of the Gospel of Luke (8:25). Seldom are such questions asked of the children and young men and women in the faith today. Why not? Perhaps it is because we have re-defined faith as being a strong, optimistic desire for something to happen. Perhaps it is because those of us in positions of spiritual leadership do not understand truly living by faith and thus cannot propagate or encourage faith living in others. Perhaps it is possible that we have lived by the flesh and gotten where we are because of our degrees, because of whom we know or whom we manipulated or because we have tickled men's ears and become popular. Whatever the reason, we should ask difficult questions of our young people so that they know where their faith is. These questions must be asked for flesh begets flesh and living by faith in the power of the Spirit begets more faith.

In the Sermon on the Mount, Jesus described the disciples as "men of little faith." In the interchange after the storm, He called the disciples "men of little faith" and also asked, "How is it that you have no faith?" Before the two-stage healing of the blind man, Jesus described the disciples again as men of little faith (Mark 8:11–26, Matthew 16:1–12). He added that they did not see or understand events that had happened over time, that their hearts were hardened, and that their hearing was very dull. In the 14th chapter of Matthew, Jesus makes a direct statement to Peter, "You of little faith, why did you doubt?" (14:31). Thus, individually and corporately, the description of the disciples' faith was "little." Like Peter, they all may have occasionally taken some steps of faith in a situation, but it is very evident (from the Sermon on the Mount to the blind man healed in stages) that the faith of the disciples was weak and sometimes not evident at all.

In contrast, the faith of the centurion (Matthew 8:5–13 and Luke 7:1–10), a Gentile, is commended as being great and unparalleled throughout all Israel. Another Gentile, a woman, besought the Lord's assistance for healing her daughter (Matthew 15:21–28 and Mark 7:24–30), and she is commended as having great faith. Some or all of the disciples were present at each of these events, and the words of Jesus should have been convicting in showing that these select Gentiles—who were not part of the religious hierarchy, who were not in the current religious system or who were not in the current popular in-group—were the individuals displaying faith. The one who walks by faith engages God and clings to His promises, no matter how contrary his situation or circumstances.

Is the greatness of the faith of these two Gentiles due to their intercession for others in their sphere of influence—the centurion for a servant and a mother for a daughter—and not themselves? One could try to make this case, but Peter's getting out of the boat to walk on the water toward Jesus discounts that conclusion. Instead, it is the active, not passive, nature of what they believed the invisible God could do in accordance to His word in their impossible circumstances. The two Gentiles did not doubt Jesus, and this was the basis of their great faith! On the other hand, Peter did not doubt initially; but on seeing the wind and most likely the resulting waves, he forgot the one word from Jesus' lips, "Come." We cannot forget the Word of God in these foreordained difficult situations and progress in the life of faith. The church and various Christian ministries today should be greenhouses for faith to flourish; but if the Word of God is not accurately handled (2 Timothy 2:15) and the shepherding of the sheep is not done in such a way to know where each sheep or lamb is, then the development of the faith of believers will be slow or counterproductive.

Jesus knew where the faith of the disciples was. He was not surprised! When our faith is stagnant, God exposes us to others who have a great faith, trying to create a thirst for a richer relationship with Him. Certainly, this is one reason why we need to read the biographies of great saints, hear the testimonies of missionaries who have seen God do great things and identify believers in the midst of our local communities who have experienced the hemming in and the deliverance by God in little and big events of life. Such things are necessary to jump-start our faith. Jesus was trying to do likewise with His disciples.

What Are Your Daily Divine Circumstances?

One could rationalize the little or weak faith of the disciples by advocating that they had no circumstances that warranted having to exercise faith. However, that reasoning is faulty because the first circumstances for which Jesus talked about faith was in the Sermon on the Mount related to food, clothing and shelter. These are the basics of life for which we have need every day. Some of us take these basics for granted, never giving thanks and glory to God for providing them, which itself is a lack of faith! Many leave God out of the picture and strive (by manipulation, coercion or other self-efforts) for sufficient daily bread or for more than is really needed. That is not the way of faith either! The path of faith is one where the focus is on the Father above, where first-order (heavenly) priorities rule and where there is no fear or worry about the future. Each day will have faith opportunities. How we respond in these daily circumstances will impact the growth or the decay of our faith. To be blind to these opportunities or moments could indicate staleness in our faith that could be extremely damaging to our souls. In fact, that staleness might require God to intervene in our "convenient" world. It is in the daily circumstances and events where one cultivates the habit of hearing the gentle voice of God.

In one such daily circumstance, Jesus said to the disciples, "Let us go over to the other side" (Mark 4:35). These words, softly communicated, came before Jesus and His disciples crossed the lake, which they had done many times previously. The failure of the disciples to truly hear and assimilate these words of Jesus led into a storm where their weak faith was exposed. In this storm, there was no focus on the Father above, no heavenly perspective, no faith and a definite fear about the circumstances including fear of possible death. This storm was critical for the disciples to see that their faith had not progressed at all. Thus, this storm had great pedagogical value to the disciples so long as they were truly teachable.

All saints will go through storms! Our faith is weak so God uses specific storms to disrupt our "convenient" world, to get our attention, to redirect our focus in life and to strengthen our faith. These storms come in the form of health problems, financial difficulties, family stresses, job strains, relational conflicts and in many other ways. Some of the greatest storms are simultaneous combinations of several of these tribulations, and they are part of the divine plan to mold and perfect our faith in a great God. We cannot choose our storms in life. God, in His infinite wisdom, knows the perfect storm and the perfect timing of that storm to perfect our faith. If we have been cultivating living by faith in the daily basics, then the likelihood of responding by faith in such storms should be much, much higher as we see that the storm has been allowed by God for divine purposes.

In the case of Peter (Matthew 14:22–33), we are exposed to another circumstance in which many young believers will find themselves. In this circumstance, the Scriptures tell us that the disciples were battered by the waves, the winds were contrary and the disciples were very tired after a long day of ministry and rowing. Upon recognizing the voice of Jesus, Peter responds to the one-word response of our Savior: "Come." The apostle took steps of faith toward Jesus, but upon seeing the wind and the waves, he evidently took his eyes off Jesus and began to sink. Peter started by faith, but he did not finish by faith. Jesus recognized that Peter exercised some faith but not enough to finish the course as evidenced by His words to Peter: "You of little faith, why did you doubt?" (Matthew 14:31).

Likewise, we may experience situations that demand faith and take the initial steps. However, the winds and waves of life distract our focus, and we begin to sink. Our Redeemer uses our failure in these kinds of circumstances to show us that walking by faith is not just a first step, but faith is to be exercised from start to finish. Faithful endurance in biblical directions is a signpost that one is maturing!

What Is the Essence of Your Faith?

This query about faith is never uniquely or explicitly spoken by Jesus toward the disciples. The explicitness of this query is captured in James 2:17–20:

> Even so faith, if it has no works, is dead, being by itself. But someone may well say, "You have faith and I have works; show me your faith without the works, and I will show you my faith by my works." You believe that God is one. You do well; the demons also believe, and shudder. But are you willing to recognize, you foolish fellow, that faith without works is useless?

Even the demons have a basic form of faith in the oneness of God, but they have no works in accordance with that basic faith. Their works are evil and do not bring glory to God. Faith that is alive and healthy is in Jesus Christ and His Word, and it produces good works that are manifested toward others.

While Jesus never asked people about the essence of their faith, He did address it twice by commending the great faith of the centurion and the Syrophoenician woman. The faith of these two individuals was very active, and it was displayed in their good deeds toward others. The centurion had built a synagogue for the Jews (Luke 7:5) and had such high regard for his slave, who was sick and about to die, that he asked others to take his petition to Jesus to come to his house to heal his slave. The Syrophoenician woman came to Jesus for her daughter, who was cruelly demon possessed. She was met with silence from Jesus, indifference from the disciples and further rebuff from Jesus. And yet sincere humility could be seen in both of these cases when the centurion said he was not worthy for Jesus to enter his house and when the Syrophoenician woman identified with the dogs that feed on the crumbs that would fall from the master's table. The centurion believed that Jesus would just have to say the word from a distance, and the servant would be healed and restored. Likewise, the woman, with her persistence, seized upon the word "first" in Jesus' words, "Let the children be satisfied first." She also believed that Jesus Christ just had to say the word and her daughter would be healed from a distance.

In both cases, there was faith in Jesus and His words. In both cases, there was true humility and a petition for another. In each case, there was perseverance needed in getting what was asked for. In both cases, they believed Jesus Christ could do the impossible from a distance so they persevered in asking. Finally, in both cases, those close to these two would have witnessed active faith. The centurion's household, the soldiers under the centurion, the Jews who had besought Jesus to come to the centurion's aid and the whole community in the centurion's sphere of influence would have had the unique testimony of this centurion's great faith. The impact of the Syrophoenician woman's faith may not have had such a far-reaching impact, but it would have impacted her household and her community.

Truly, Jesus Christ is "the author and perfecter of faith" (Hebrews 12:2), but it is obvious that what He does in perfecting our faith does not stay behind closed doors. Rather, it is a unique testimony to others who may be watching. In addition, the effect of our faith maturing may have a great impact on many people, as in the case of the centurion, or the impact could be on just a few, as may have been the case for the Syrophoenician woman. "For we are His workmanship, created in Christ Jesus for good works, which God prepared beforehand so that we would walk in them" (Ephesians 2:10). As we so do, we leave the results to God, which is also part of walking by faith!

What Are Your Repeat Circumstances?

If believers were perfect learners and appliers of biblical truth, there would be no need for repeat experiences. However, we all have blind spots, hardness of heart, baggage from our pre-Christian years or from recurring sin patterns and corrupted thinking from the world or the flesh that hinders us from incorporating biblical truth into our lives by faith. As a result, the Author and Finisher of our faith sovereignly allows or arranges repeat experiences, frequently with a different façade, to test our faith and to aid the progression of that faith.

In the case of the disciples, during their first year or two with Jesus, there were three sets of repeat experiences: those on the boat, those providing or centering on bread and those commending great faith. The first set of repeats as to the boat experiences was similar but also dissimilar. The first boat experience came after the commendation of the great faith of the centurion and after a deep teaching time (Mark 4:1–34), while the second boat experience with Peter walking on the water seems to have been within six months of the first boat experience but right after the feeding of the five thousand (John 6:1–15).

Each of these boat experiences came after a time of great revelation and great faith. In the first boat experience it seemed to be a life-and-death situation yet it was not. Jesus reprimanded them for having little faith, queried them as to where their faith was and commented that they had displayed no faith in this first boat experience. In the second boat experience, the disciples were tired and the winds and waves were contrary, but at least Peter took some initial steps of faith. He just doubted when he saw the wind and waves and accordingly took his eyes off of Jesus. There is some progression in faith by Peter in this set of repeat experiences but the faith was not sustained, and the end result of unsustained faith was failure.

The second set of repeat experiences centered on bread. There was the feeding of the five thousand, the feeding of the four thousand and the later discussion among the disciples that they had no bread (Mark 8:14-26). The disciples should have learned that Jesus Christ was all-sufficient for whatever need they had. They saw Jesus provide food two times before, they even participated in the distribution and collection of the food. Yet they did not understand or even remember the issues surrounding the All-Sufficient One and His provision for the people. They could not make the transference of truth and faith from one instance to another, and that is why Jesus implied that they may have a hardened heart and directly identified them as "men of little faith" (Matthew 16:8). Jesus uses this failure in this set of repeat experiences to point out that faith comes in stages. Despite being close to Jesus, the disciples were acting like children in the faith in that they were only seeing partially and not wholly!

The last set of repeat experiences revolved around commendation of the great faith of both the centurion and the Syrophoenician woman. The great faith of the centurion was praised just prior to the storm on the sea, and Peter's failure to walk on the sea was just prior to the great faith of the Syrophoenician woman. Both of these situations should have pierced the souls and minds of the disciples, but seemingly they did not at the time. The two commended for great faith were Gentiles, not Jews—one was a man and the other a woman. Thus, great faith is not limited by race, gender, vocation, location or station in life.

Common features between the centurion's story and the one of the Syrophoenician woman went beyond just great faith. First, they were both very humble before God and men. There is no indication in Scripture that the centurion or the Syrophoenician woman argued with others about who was the greatest, the way the disciples frequently did. Second, they both were in impossible situations, and they saw Jesus as the only answer. Third, whereas the disciples missed the words, "Let us go to the other side" of the lake or "Come" as spoken to Peter, the centurion and the Syrophoenician woman seized the words coming from the lips of Jesus and applied them to their situations rightly. Fourth, these two people with great faith were very other-focused in their sphere of influence. Their faith represented not just words but actions on behalf of others. It is very difficult for faith to blossom if there is not a focus on others around us at home, in the neighborhood, at work or in the community.

Life Response to Biblical Truth
1. We all need to be challenged to answer the questions: Where is your faith? What are your cir-

cumstances? What is the essence of your faith? What are your repeat experiences? Answers to these queries will reveal how far we have yet to go in the Lord. These are queries we need to ask of ourselves in the power of the Holy Spirit at least several times a year. If our communication with the Lord is vibrant and if we talk with Him and listen to Him daily, then such questions may come from the lips of the Lord or others more frequently. These questions should also be asked by those in leadership of the people they are shepherding. The shepherds should know where the sheep are in the faith, not from guess-work but from a relational closeness.

2. Much of the time Jesus described the faith of the disciples as "little." Occasionally, He said they had no faith at all. Believers need deep teaching from the Word, rich personal Bible study, moment-by-moment prayer with the Father and fruitful application of the truths received into the daily life—all in the power of the Holy Spirit. Mark 4:24–25 records these words from Jesus: "Take care what you listen to. By your standard of measure it will be measured to you; and more shall be given you besides. For who-ever has, to him more shall be given; and who-ever does not have, even what he has shall be taken away from him." If we do not assimilate the truth that we hear, we will lose the truth that we thought we had. The end result is that we do

not progress in our faith and our senses are not trained to discern good and evil (Hebrews 5:14). Also, some experiences seem to always be repeating, and we continue to partake of spiritual milk while we stay babes in the faith (Hebrews 5:13). Babes in Christ are not going to change the world!

3. How do we jump-start our faith if we seem to be in a rut? Of course, we can read the stories of saints in the past, such as Hudson Taylor, Dwight Moody and others who displayed faith in a great God. We can identify people and learn from people in our local communities who have illustrated faith. We can be sure we're sitting under solid, biblical teaching. All of these things will help, but most important is to love our Father in heaven more by being obedient to His Word. As we are obedient, our faith will begin to grow. However, this growth is very, very slow in a vacuum. The fertile soil for this growth to mature is deep relationships with other believers, where there is accountability, submission and ministry. Where is your faith? Do you honestly know?

4. Our God is not distant! He is concerned about our daily walk with Him, and He wants that walk to bring glory to Himself and Himself alone. The circumstances of daily life are the potential fertile grounds for our faith to flour-

ish or blossom. The circumstances are divinely allowed, ordained and ordered. God is the Master Artist who is using all things in our life to mature our faith in Him. If we respond in these circumstances with self-effort, fleshy schemes, manipulations, indifference or anything besides faith, then we have missed an opportunity to trust God, to know Him better and to grow out of the child's-level faith stage. We must begin where we are and allow God to transform our lives in a magnificent way!

5. If daily life is filled with noise, hustle and diverse worldly stimulations, we won't be able to be still and hear the voice of God. As a result, we can be sure that God will use storms to capture our attention. We need to be very careful when these storms come. If we are not in a teachable mood when they come, God in His infinite love for us will use more intense or more frequent storms to move our focus toward Him as being all-sufficient. The storms may not look the same in all circumstances, but they have been divinely allowed to move our faith out of the stagnancy of being little. These situations demand that we have mature believers who can see what God is doing and speak into our lives with suggestions, counsel or encouragement.

6. All believers go through storms, and many of those storms are life threatening or life changing. These storms should be springboards for our faith as we apply the Scriptures. It is true that the purpose of the storm could be discipline for "He disciplines us for our good, so that we may share His holiness" (Hebrews 12:10). In such storms, we should repent and reflect on how we have departed from God's Word in order to restore our faith. But no matter what the purpose of the storm, a nonbiblical response will undermine our faith and not mature it.

7. Faith that is well produces good toward God and others. The soil that produces thirty, sixty or a hundredfold must be sprinkled with humility, prayer for others, perseverance in light of the promises and belief that God can do the impossible. He may not so do, but He can! True faith displayed God's way is veiled and impacts others, as in the case of the centurion and the Syrophoenician woman.

8. Jesus' interactions with the disciples about their faith reveals that today's shepherds—whether pastor, elder, small group leader or mentor— must know where others are in their faith. No pastor can know the state of faith for five hundred people in his congregation. However, if the counsel of Jethro to Moses in Exodus 18 is taken seriously, where we have leaders of tens, fifties,

hundreds and thousands, a pastor could have an excellent sense of where the faith of the sheep is from the discipling leadership in the church. One of our difficulties in today's church or ministries is that leadership is too often based on the successful corporate model, which is not faith based. As such, there are people in leadership positions who are weak in faith and even some who have no faith. All of those in leadership positions need to ask themselves, "Where is my faith?" At the same time, Jesus knew where the faith of the twelve disciples was, and He was very effective at revealing it to them. Instead of operating on the corporate model, should we not also consider the small group model that Jesus perfected to monitor and mature the faith of others?

Questions for Reflection

1. Do you have intimate discipling or mentoring re-
    lationships with other believers that could ask you
    questions about your faith, your circumstances and
    your repeat experiences? Do you have such relation-
    ships with other believers where you could address
    such things with them? How does one move into
    this shepherding or discipling process? Why is this
    so important to our faith?

2. What are the sources of biblical input that you have
    during the week? Which source is the richest and
    most meaningful to you? Explain why. Which source
    should be the richest, and why?

3. "Everyone who has been given much, much will be
    required" (Luke 12:48). What does this mean as to
    truth and faith?

4. Have you noticed God-ordained storms in your
    life over the past few years? List the stormy events.
    What commonalities did they have? What did you
    learn about God? What do you think your shep-

herd or discipler would say that you should have learned?

5. A diet of "milk," no discernment, little faith and busyness apart from God, indicate what stage of faith? God is the One who takes us through these stages of faith. What has God been doing in your life over the past year to make you uncomfortable where you are and to increase your desire for a closer relationship with Him by faith?

6. Has God seemed distant lately? What could be some of the reasons for this distant feeling? Depending upon the reason, what should your response be?

7. There is a lot of divine good that comes from these God-ordained storms. What good has come out of your storms?

8. Jesus used His small group of twelve to monitor, challenge and mature the faith of the disciples. Where does one find such small groups that do likewise?

Chapter 14

Hard Issues about Faith

In Chapter 7, we highlighted the blind man who was healed in stages. The implication from that miracle is that there are stages in the Christian life, either as the child, young person or the father in the faith (1 John 2:12–14) or as the blade, the head and then the mature grain in the head (Mark 4:26–29). As a believer presses on in the life of faith or aspires to move to a higher stage of maturity, there will come time for some hard lessons. These hard lessons will cover failure, the realization that one's faith is not where it should be, the recognition that not many around you in your sphere of influence are walking by faith or even desirous of so doing, a greater consciousness of the strengths of the flesh and severe testing of your faith.

These types of experiences are necessary for our faith to be proven more precious than gold. However, we may try to engineer these moments on our own, but the results will not last. These experiences are divinely arranged and timed by God to mature our faith. As we rest in the sovereignty of God and respond to His Word and the leading of His Spirit in these experiences, we will progress in faith.

Significant Failure and Faith

Truly, the three disciples failed to realize the significance of the moment on the Mount of Transfiguration with Jesus while the other nine disciples failed miserably in casting out a demon from a father's son while in the valley of service to others. These were not the first failures the disciples experienced, nor would they be the last! There were at least three other failures: in a storm, in walking on water and in a repeated experience with bread. In the storm on the sea (Matthew 8:18–27; Mark 4:36–41; and Luke 8:22–25), the disciples in total failed miserably as evidenced by Jesus' words, "Where is your faith?" in Luke 8:25 and "Do you still have no faith?" in Mark 4:40.

The second instance involved Peter walking on the water by faith, but on seeing the wind he began to sink (Matthew 14:24–33). He too had failed as evidenced by Jesus' words to him, "You of little faith, why did you doubt?" The third instance is recorded in Mark 8:11-25. In the feeding of the five thousand and the feeding of the four thousand, Jesus tried to help the disciples understand that He is sufficient for every need. He again called the disciples "men of little faith" (Matthew 16:8) and after recounting events for them asked, "Do you not yet understand?" (Mark 8:21). Thus, it is very obvious that the disciples had failed much in deed and in faith during Jesus' tenure of ministry.

What do we learn from these failures and faith as recorded in the Gospels? As to the current reality, we live in a culture that praises, rewards and envies success but treats failure as a cancer to be avoided at all costs. However, these failures by the disciples were servants of the most High God (Psalm 119:91), and there is much to be learned from them for our good. First, in each case of failure Jesus noted the littleness or the lack of faith. He did not harp on the failure but stated the obvious and moved on. He did not throw up past failures in their face but dealt with the situation before them. We need to ask ourselves if we are in tune to the voice of God as He speaks from the Scriptures. Are we in tune to God's voice when spoken through one of His servants as he or she points out a weakness or failure in our lives? It is natural for us to ignore such warnings or rebuke unless they come from an accepted source. The book of Proverbs says, "Reprove a wise man and he will love you" (9:8). Rarely is such reproof expressed that highlights our little or lacking faith. We should be grateful when it is.

Second, Jesus seemed to be gentle, gracious and forgiving of the disciples when they failed. If we are honest with ourselves before God, we have all failed in the past and will all fail in endeavors to come if we do not trust the Savior completely. Many of our failures are actually our "perceived successes" as in the case of Moses getting water from the rock the second time by striking it instead of speaking to it (Numbers 20). Outwardly, in that case, the moment seemed to be a success since water was provided for the people and animals. Yet privately Moses was reprimanded for not treating God as holy before the congregation of Israel. The ultimate discipline was not being able to go into the Promised Land.

We will all fail in all sorts of ways (in ventures, in moments, in relationships, in activities or programs, in jobs) for we are not perfect. We have blind spots. We start by faith but end up finishing in the power of the flesh. On many other occasions, we start by the flesh and finish by the flesh—and we want God to bless what we do. God longs to be gracious to us, and God forgives us if we confess; but He wants us to learn from our failures and not consider the failures successes. As we learn, we will grow in faith and grace!

Third, the first three failures occurred in the small company of the disciples and Jesus, but the last failure (see Chapter 7) on the Mount of Transfiguration and in the valley of life occurred before the Father and the prophets and the public, respectively. There were obvious consequences for their lack of faith this time. On the Mount of Transfiguration, there was a reprimand from the Father, "This is My Beloved Son, listen to Him." In the valley, there was public embarrassment, and there would have been potential dishonor to the name and ministry of Jesus Christ if the Savior had not sovereignly arrived at the right moment to correct the failure of the nine disciples.

The consequences of earlier failures seemed to be minimal to the disciples while this last failure exposed the reality that their faith was very weak, as it had been the whole time of our Lord's ministry. Even minor failures, however, for which there are no obvious consequences, are extremely damaging to the life of faith in that it is human nature to play the "what if" or the "next time" game of manipulating events and people to get the desired success in the next situation. Hearts that are continually tender toward the Lord and His word will confess the fleshy efforts and wait on Him, His way and His timing. To do otherwise is to digress in faith and to miss the richness of walking closely with our Savior.

Fourth, Jesus always saw potential in people, even in spite of their failures. Remember while the Lord knew that Peter would deny Him three times and that the disciples would desert Him, He still prayed for them that their faith would not fail. In addition, He prayed that Peter would strengthen his brothers and sisters in Christ once he returned to the Lord. These failures that the disciples went through were tools in the hands of a loving God to break these men, to mold and expand their faith and to equip them to teach and to disciple others in the realm of faith. God, in His infinite wisdom, knew what it would take to make these few men truly men of God. It would take failure for their faith to blossom!

Increased Faith

After two years with Jesus in ministry, the disciples had approached Jesus with a request: "Increase our faith!" (Luke 17:5). They saw at least thirty miracles during these two years of ministry, and they had been in the inner circle of the hottest ministry of their day and of all time. Yet they experienced failures in their walks of faith. The littleness of their faith had not become paramount to them until Jesus talked about relationships with others and the seventy times seven expansive nature of forgiveness. They immediately recognized that they could not forgive like God forgave. They did not have the resources within themselves to forgive the divine way. Their conclusion was that they needed more faith and that there should be some magic formula (which there is not) for that increased faith.

For the disciples, Jesus' words on forgiveness were a trigger point in their walk of faith, which revealed their faith as deficient. They immediately recognized that they needed more faith than they had. Sad to say, most saints don't come to this realization as quickly as the disciples did. This realization comes through trigger points or precipitating events or crises in life or just natural events in life processes, such as college graduation, marriage, birth of a first child, a close encounter with death, death of a parent or just aging. If Christians are in tune to the living God, the Father will use these events to remind us that we are unable within ourselves to live this Christian life of faith. We desperately need Him in it all!

The disciples were taught that faith is predicated on moment-by-moment obedience to the Word of God and the Lord Himself. That obedience is to be tempered with thanksgiving, humility and waiting on Him for further instructions as illustrated by only one of the ten blind men returning to Jesus (Luke 17:11–19). It is this one blind man, a Samaritan, who gained in faith because he came back to Jesus, giving thanks and glorifying God. Every day we have opportunities for obedience, and those opportunities should drive us back to the feet of Jesus, thanking Him for His ways, glorifying His name and waiting for His next words to us. As we miss these daily opportunities to walk in obedience and faith, it will take more intense crises to capture our attention and teach us that our faith is weak. It will take more to nudge us to return to Jesus giving more thanks, further glorifying His name, spending more time in His Word and basking in His presence in such a way that is not a forced relationship.

Our omniscient Father in heaven knows the types of events, the timings of these events and the sequences of these precipitating events that each of us needs to realize where our faith is and how much more faith we need in Him. It took two years or more for the disciples to come to that point. It should be great comfort to the individual believer that our loving Father has chosen these trigger events uniquely for us. His hand and His love are exhibited by the type, intensity and timing of these divinely ordained events for the individual believer. To overlook these events is to reject God's best, to miss the opportunity for our faith to blossom and to miss the chance to know Him better.

Presence of Faith

In the progression of faith, Jesus' words, "When the Son of Man comes, will He find faith on the earth?" (Luke 18:8), follow the failure of faith and the request for increased faith. If we don't learn from our mistakes and failures or if the precipitating events of life don't drive us to our knees, asking for more faith and increased obedience to the Lord, then the likelihood of finding faith on earth becomes less likely over time. Of course, while it is true that there is always a remnant in each generation that only bows the knee to Jesus Christ, it is most likely that this remnant will become even smaller over time.

What are the signs of this waning faith? In the parable about the wicked judge and the widow in the 18th chapter of Luke, Jesus mentioned to the disciples the need to pray at all times, to not lose heart and to persist in asking (Luke 18:1–8). The saint who doesn't realize his or her need to pray at all times moves his or her generation closer to exercising less faith and dilutes the norms of Christian experience in the following generation. For many, the norms of experience become the benchmark rather than the Word of God. The believer who prays at all times recognizes that nothing can be done apart from the Lord (John 15:5) and that we must abide in Christ moment by moment. That dependent relationship permeates all that the individual believer does in all spheres of life—at home, at work and in the community. To pray at all times in the Spirit (Ephesians 6:18) is the norm of the Christian life for every believer, not just a select few who are thought to be "prayer warriors." Believers who pray in this manner will grow in their faith because dramatic events, trials and opportunities will prod them to ask the Father how to respond. Do they respond with biblical action right then, wait until tomorrow or just wait on the Lord for Him to do what He wants to do in His way and His time? This kind of prayer life is enriching communion with the Father that always results in increased faith.

A second sign of waning faith is the ease of losing heart. Without question, believers desiring to mature in the faith may lose heart from time to time in ministry (2 Corinthians 4:1), in doing good (Galatians 6:9), in trials (Ephesians 3:13) or in the decay of the outer man (2 Corinthians 4:16). There is a lot in life that can cause a believer to lose heart. However, if we fix our eyes "on Jesus, the author and perfecter of faith" (Hebrews 12:2) and His Word, then we will realize that the experiences or events that are causing us to lose heart are from the loving hands of our Father in heaven, meant to mature us in the faith. We need to see as He sees and to trust Him when we cannot see as He sees.

To trust Him when we cannot see as He sees requires us knowing Him more deeply in a daily way. As a result over time, the tendency to lose heart in ministry, in doing good, in trials or in the decay of the outer man will become less and our faith will become greater. On the other hand, if the saint does not see as God sees or cannot trust Him for what he or she cannot see, then this person rationalizes the experiences or events as bad luck, as being at the wrong place at the wrong time, as being someone else's fault or as being any explanation that leaves God out of the equation. The end result of this sequence is less walking by faith, more need to be continually pumped up emotionally and a weakened faith throughout a generation. Thus, when He returns, will He find faith on the earth?

The third sign of waning faith is lack of persistence in asking, which is partly a by-product of not praying at all times, losing heart and not knowing the Word of God and our Savior well enough. If we truly understood that our gracious God is not like the wicked judge in the parable of Luke 18:1–6, then we might persist in asking more, and our faith would grow more. God is willing to hear and to act in His time upon our requests because He loves us and wants the best for us. The saints must have a practical and vibrant daily understanding of His character for our faith to have a chance to grow. On the other hand, believers must also understand that when one becomes a Christian, he does not gain entrance into the local holy country club. Instead, we are adopted into God's family and enlisted in His army. Our adversary, the devil, is real! The conflicts that Christians experience with the world and the flesh need to be won in Christ and not ignored as trivial and insignificant. We are in a battle for the hearts, minds and souls of people as well as a battle for our faith. This battle isn't obvious to most, but the one walking in faith knows that he or she is helpless, must cling to the Father and must stand on the promises of God in the power of the Holy Spirit to have a chance to experience the victory. When one knows the Word of God and the promises therein, he or she has substance or support for asking, can persist in asking and less likelihood of losing heart.

A troubling sign of our time is poor and power-less teaching and preaching from the Word of God in our churches and ministries. When the Word is taught lightly and without seriousness, it can be so accented with examples, stories, philosophy or psychological babble that the truths, especially the deep truths, are watered down with little value for daily, Spirit-filled living. While this may be true in our generation, each believer is still responsible to study the Word, pray at all times, walk in the power of the Holy Spirit by faith and be faithful in what God has called us to accomplish. Again, there will always be a remnant that will walk by faith; but when a generation of believers does not know the Word of God and their Savior well, the ability to persist in asking of God and walking by faith will decrease even more in the next genera-tion unless the Lord God intervenes. The question again is, "Will He find faith on the earth?" The number of the faith-based believers will diminish the closer we get to the last days but not the qual-ity of believers.

Faith in God

We need to hear "Have faith in God" every day. In addition, our days need to have time for reflec-tion under the power of the Holy Spirit where we try to assess whether or not we walked by faith that day. It is extremely natural to trust in anything or anybody but God. The prophet Isaiah said: "Woe to those who go down to Egypt for help and rely on horses, and trust in chariots because they are many and in horsemen because they are very strong, but they do not look to the Holy One of Israel, nor seek the LORD" (31:1).

Israel's trust was continually being misplaced as they put confidence in Egypt, horses, chariots and horsemen (the professionals and power brokers of their day) instead of the Lord. Believers do the same today as we trust in institutions, the current power brokers, the professionals, the man-made tools of our day and people. It seems that nothing has changed as God's people look to Him or seek Him, only as a last resort. It is no wonder that progress in the life of faith is so very slow!

For almost three years, Jesus observed the faith walk of the disciples. There were occasional moments of faith, but the continuum of walking by faith was not outwardly evident. As a result, Jesus sought to create a teachable moment by cursing the fig tree during His last week before the cross. His teaching to the disciples was "to have faith in God" and with that kind of faith they could cast mountains into the sea. "Faith comes from hearing, and hearing by the word of Christ" (Romans 10:17), but the disciples had not been hearing His words about His death and resurrection to come (at least three times), nor had they detected the pattern in the three resurrections that Jesus had performed. All the evidences of His words were before them, but for whatever reason, they did not grasp these truths.

In this perfectly timed teachable moment, Jesus used the cursing of the fig tree to see if the hearts and minds of the disciples could pick up an obvious divine pattern in daily life. They did! Jesus noted that their response to His words and their response to forgiving others and even themselves could undermine having faith in God. The example of the fig tree and the mountains here was no coincidence. It is possible to scheme and use the institutions, technology and power brokers of our day to get what we want and leave God out. That is possible with fig trees but not with mountains! Living by faith is living without scheming, manipulation and deception.

On the other hand, Jesus either sensed or expected that the disciples, who started by faith in God, would never mature in their faith until He was gone. This command "to have faith in God" was critical because of the tendencies human nature has to build trust in other things or people over time. The words of A.W. Tozer reflect this point:

> Schleiermacher has pointed out at the bottom of all religion there lies a feeling of dependence, a sense of creature helplessness. The simple man who lives close to the earth lives also close to death and knows that he must look for help beyond himself; he knows that there is but a step between him and catastrophe. As he rises in the social and economic scale, he surrounds himself with more and more protective devices and pushes

danger (so he thinks) farther and farther from him. Self-confidence displaces the feeling of dependence he once knew and God becomes less necessary to him. Should he stop to think this through he would know better than to place his confidence in things and people; but so badly are we injured by the moral fall that we are capable of deceiving ourselves completely and, if conditions favor it, to keep up the deception for a lifetime.[1]

Thus, we as believers try to insulate or protect ourselves with many devices that may be gifts from God; but these may undermine our faith because we trust in the gifts and not the Giver of the gifts. The end result is deception about our faith and our true relationship to the Father through the Son. Sad to say, we are seeing believers today who have been involved in this deception for a lifetime, and it is difficult for such a deceived generation to pass on their faith in Him when it has been misplaced in things or others.

The other deception that undermines our faith in God is our sinfulness. We can use these same gifts from God to inflate our hearts and convince our minds that we are worthy of such gifts because of our great walk with God. As a result of our perceived worth, the deceived mind believes that when we are wronged, we have a right to hold a grudge or that the other persons were wrong and should ask forgiveness from us. The whole reality of relationships with others is distorted, and the ability to have faith in a great God becomes impossible. This is why we need to ask God to search our hearts and thoughts daily (Psalm 139:23). A by-product of that daily process is forgiveness toward others and an increased faith in a great God. May we remember the humility, thanksgiving and worship of one Samaritan leper as he focused on the Giver of gifts and not the gift itself!

Failed Faith and Faith Restored

The pattern of faith in the disciples during the years with our Lord seems difficult to discern. It could have been up and down, weak or strong, little or nonexistent—but it was almost always inconsistent. In the field of statistics, there is the area of time series analysis where one tries to discover the patterns in time sequenced data. The most difficult pattern to determine is one that not only looks at today's result as a function of previous periods but that is a weighted average of an individual's deviations from walking God's way in times past.

The implication to believers is that our faith is not only impacted by our choices in critical or monumental events but also by our exercise of faith in a daily way in normal situations. Our Lord knew that the faith of the disciples was not where it needed to be to carry on the ministry He committed to them. He knew that they would deny Him and desert Him and that their faith could fail. They did not know that they would fail Him, but they needed to know it if they were going to help others in the life of faith.

In light of what Jesus knew about the faith of the disciples, He challenged and instructed them to have faith in God during His last week with them. In His last hours, He bluntly told Peter and the rest that "Satan has demanded permission to sift you like wheat; but I have prayed for you that your faith may not fail and you, when you have turned again, strengthen your brothers."

When our faith is not where it should be and when we are ill equipped in faith in Christ to handle the divine tasks God has for us, severe testing of our faith is necessary for spiritual progress. God will use whatever or whomever He needs to use to refine our faith. Whatever He does or whomever He uses might shake us to the very core of our being. He has allowed these situations to prove our faith (1 Peter 1:7), to help us to understand where our faith is or is not and to redirect our focus onto Him alone. He knows that Satan will try to use whatever or whomever to destroy our faith, but what God has allowed to occur is to prove the worth of our faith (which is "more precious than gold, which is perishable," 1 Peter 1:7). What God allowed for the disciples could have caused their faith to fail completely, but what God allows is always balanced by the constant intercession of our Savior on our behalf (Hebrews 7:25).

This severe testing of the disciples and their subsequent failure of deserting Jesus could not be avoided. It had been predicted in Zechariah 13:7, so it was certain to happen. On the other hand, this sifting of their faith was not only to purify and mature the faith of these disciples but also to inform future disciples that God does allow the bottom to drop out of our lives and dreams. When that happens, we may be crushed with a sense of uselessness and hopelessness and even a sense that God does not care.

After their desertion of Him, the disciples felt it all when Jesus was tried, sentenced to the cross, crucified and buried in the tomb. The crash of their expectations, the weakness of their faith and the hopelessness of the situation was surely felt for three days. But when the news was received from the women that the Lord had been raised and when the disciples realized the news was true, their faith was restored and forever changed. Their faith was sight; and as Jesus had prayed for them, it did not fail. It is important to note, however, that the sovereign God allows the severe testing, the accompanying darkness of it and the absence of the sensed presence of God to move us into a deeper relationship with Him and into a richer faith. The others-oriented result of this severe testing was that the disciples would be able to strengthen the saints exactly as Jesus had prayed!

Concluding Comments on Faith

Much more could be said, but there comes a time in the life of every believer where he or she needs to listen and learn from the Lord directly in the matters of faith. More words, more teaching and more applications about faith do not assist the believer in living by faith unless he or she is striving in the power of the Holy Spirit to walk by faith. The proof of this is obvious in our Gospel study of the little or sometimes nonexistent faith of the disciples. However, the principle is also conveyed in the Old Testament when the people responded to Moses, "Speak to us yourself and we will listen; but let not God speak to us, or we will die" (Exodus 20:19). When someone else speaks the truth to us, we discount their words and say that it is their interpretation; and thus we rationalize that we are not accountable. On the other hand, when we have heard it directly from the Lord (whether from another speaker or from our own study in the Scriptures or from circumstances), our perspective of God is greatly magnified and our inability to obey His words without His help is heightened. The net result is that our faith in Him grows more! As a result of this phenomenon, the life responses are purposely omitted from this chapter so that individual readers can prove their own faithfulness before God and their faith can grow more!

One day our faith will be sight, but until that day, we need to press on in the activities of faith:

study of the Word, prayer, doing good toward others, sharing the good news of salvation and walking daily with our Savior. We may not be able to assess where our faith is at this moment. Is it the faith of a child, a young man or woman or an adult (1 John 2:13–14)? This assessment may be difficult to make by one's own, but God will reveal it in His time. However, the most likely course is the assumption that our faith walk is at the lowest level, that of a child.

From Ecclesiastes 3:1, "There is an appointed time for everything." There is a time for repetition of truths for the purpose of reinforcing the faith of the believer or enriching the worship of believers. There is also a time for deeper truths that challenge our faith. There is a time for each! However, as to the heart, do we crave hearing the elementary truths of Scripture so that we feel that we have arrived? Do we realize that "heavy" repetition of the elementary truths of the faith dulls the spiritual faculties of believers? Do we love to hear a few basic doctrines over and over so that we are not made uncomfortable? Tozer has some deep things to say about this:

> The teaching that consists entirely of reiteration cannot but be dull and wearisome; so the churches [and ministries, my words] try to make up for the religious lassitude they cannot help by introducing extra-scriptural diversions and anti-scriptural entertainments to provide the stultified saints with a bit of relish for their

tedium. It never seems to occur to anyone that there is true joy farther on if they would only escape from the circle and strike out for the hills of God. To bring news already known; to marshal texts to prove truth everyone believes and no one disputes; to illustrate by endless stores doctrines long familiar; to lay again and again the foundations of repentance from dead works and faith toward God—this is to labor the obvious. "Therefore leaving the principles of the doctrine of Christ, let us go on unto perfection (Hebrews 6:1)."[2]

It is a dangerous place to stay at the level of a babe in the faith. Believers need accountability in the body of Christ. They need shepherding, solid food from the Word of God and faith in God. We cannot allow believers to hide in our congregations or ministries, not to have true shepherds who are concerned for the spiritual welfare of the sheep, to receive watered-down or shallow truths and to wallow in their quagmire of stagnancy in faith. To allow this state of chaos affects the next generation of believers.

For those who seriously want to progress in the life of faith, be sure that Jesus, the Author and Perfecter of faith, will move us there. He will use setbacks, reversals, disappointments, failure, trials and many other things as He ministers to accomplish His will in our lives. We even may have more failure than success as we realize that some of our perceived successes were failures in that we left God out. We will realize that we need more faith and that we need to cling to Him more than ever before. This realization of the need for increased faith will be triggered by unique events designed sovereignly for us to realize or to be honest with ourselves that our faith is seriously lacking. As we are sensitized by God for increased faith, we will be made more aware of our surroundings, relationships, deeds and interactions where faith is not being exercised. And this, in turn, will help us see how frequently we place faith in anything or anyone but God. As we understand and confess our misplaced faith and look to Jesus Christ and His Word with obedience in the power of the Holy Spirit, then our faith will begin to grow; and our communion with the Father in heaven will become richer.

The life of faith is not a bed of roses! God may allow us to be sifted by Satan as was done with the disciples. We must always remember that God's allowance of Satan to work is always bounded with constraints so that the testing of our faith will prove the quality of it. We must also remember that Jesus is making intercession for us in such times and that God's purposes for such testing are not only for the refining of our faith, but also that the experiences might equip us to comfort and to minister to others more effectively and powerfully. All that God allows to come our way springs out of His love for us and His desire to see us "walk by faith, not by sight" (2 Corinthians 5:7).

Author's Note

My prayer for those who have recently come to Christ is that they will mature in the Lord and grow in their faith. For those who have known Christ as their Savior for a much longer time but may have become stagnant in their walk of faith, I pray for brokenness, repentance and a fresh renewing of heart and mind to be more like Christ. For those of you who have been faithful to the Lord over the years, may you excel still more in faith and love.

No matter where you are in the life of faith, may the Word of God and the truths pieced together from the Gospels in this book create joy and excitement in walking by faith with our great God. As your faith is invigorated by God alone, may you feel the burden of passing on the baton of faith to the next generation. And finally, may we each study deeply the Lord Jesus Christ's words and ways in the Gospels so as not to forget His priorities and His interest in our faith in Him!

APPENDIX
Scriptures on Faith

Romans 1:5 Through whom we have received grace and apostleship to bring about the obedience of faith among all the Gentiles for His name's sake.

Romans 1:8 First, I thank my God through Jesus Christ for you all, because your faith is being proclaimed throughout the whole world.

Romans 1:12 That is, that I may be encouraged together with you while among you, each of us by the other's faith, both yours and mine.

Romans 1:17 For in it the righteousness of God is revealed from faith to faith; as it is written, "BUT THE RIGHTEOUS man SHALL LIVE BY FAITH."

Romans 3:3 What then? If some did not believe, their unbelief will not nullify the faithfulness of God, will it?

Romans 3:22 Even the righteousness of God through faith in Jesus Christ for all those who believe; for there is no distinction.

Romans 3:25 Whom God displayed publicly as a propitiation in His blood through faith. This was to demonstrate His righteousness, because in the forbearance of God He passed over the sins previously committed.

Romans 3:26 For the demonstration, I say, of His righteousness at the present time, so that He would be just and the justifier of the one who has faith in Jesus.

Romans 3:27 Where then is boasting? It is excluded. By what kind of law? Of works? No, but by a law of faith.

Romans 3:28 For we maintain that a man is justified by faith apart from works of the Law.

Romans 3:30 Since indeed God who will justify the circumcised by faith and the uncircumcised through faith is one.

Romans 3:31 Do we then nullify the Law through faith? May it never be! On the contrary, we establish the Law.

Romans 4:5 But to the one who does not work, but believes in Him who justifies the ungodly, his faith is credited as righteousness.

Romans 4:9 Is this blessing then on the circumcised, or on the uncircumcised also? For we say, "FAITH WAS CREDITED TO ABRAHAM AS RIGHTEOUSNESS."

Romans 4:11 And [Abraham] received the sign of circumcision, a seal of the righteousness of the faith which he had while uncircumcised, so that he might be the father of all who believe without being circumcised, that righteousness might be credited to them.

Romans 4:12 And the father of circumcision to those who not only are of the circumcision, but who also follow in the steps of the faith of our father Abraham which he had while uncircumcised.

Romans 4:13 For the promise to Abraham or to his descendants that he would be heir of the world was not through the Law, but through the righteousness of faith.

Romans 4:14 For if those who are of the Law are heirs, faith is made void and the promise is nullified.

Romans 4:16 For this reason it is by faith, in order that it may be in accordance with grace, so that the promise will be guaranteed to all the descendants, not only to those who are of the Law, but also to those who are of the faith of Abraham, who is the father of us all.

Romans 4:19 Without becoming weak in faith he contemplated his own body, now as good as dead since he was about a hundred years old, and the deadness of Sarah's womb.

Romans 4:20 Yet, with respect to the promise of God, he did not waver in unbelief but grew strong in faith, giving glory to God.

Romans 5:1 Therefore, having been justified by faith, we have peace with God through our Lord Jesus Christ.

Romans 5:2 Through whom also we have obtained our introduction by faith into this grace in which we stand; and we exult in hope of the glory of God.

Romans 9:30 What shall we say then? That Gentiles, who did not pursue righteousness, attained righteousness, even the righteousness which is by faith.

Romans 9:32 Why? Because they did not pursue it by faith, but as though it were by works. They stumbled over the stumbling stone.

Romans 10:6 But the righteousness based on faith speaks as follows: "DO NOT SAY IN YOUR HEART, 'WHO WILL ASCEND INTO HEAVEN?' (that is, to bring Christ down).

Romans 10:8 But what does it say? "THE WORD IS NEAR YOU, IN YOUR MOUTH AND IN YOUR HEART"—that is, the word of faith which we are preaching.

Romans 10:17 So faith comes from hearing, and hearing by the word of Christ.

Romans 11:20 Quite right, they were broken off for their unbelief, but you stand by your faith. Do not be conceited, but fear.

Romans 12:3 For through the grace given to me I say to everyone among you not to think more highly of himself than he ought to think; but to think so as to have sound judgment, as God has allotted to each a measure of faith.

Romans 12:6 Since we have gifts that differ according to the grace given to us, each of us is to exercise them accordingly: if prophecy, according to the proportion of his faith.

Romans 14:1 Now accept the one who is weak in faith, but not for the purpose of passing judgment on his opinions.

Romans 14:2 One person has faith that he may eat all things, but he who is weak eats vegetables only.

Romans 14:22 The faith which you have, have as your own conviction before God. Happy is he who does not condemn himself in what he approves.

Romans 14:23 But he who doubts is condemned if he eats, because his eating is not from faith; and whatever is not from faith is sin.

Romans 16:26 But now is manifested, and by the Scriptures of the prophets, according to the commandment of the eternal God, has been made known to all the nations, leading to obedience of faith.

1 Corinthians 2:5 That your faith would not rest on the wisdom of men, but on the power of God.

1 Corinthians 12:9 To another faith by the same Spirit, and to another gifts of healing by the one Spirit.

1 Corinthians 13:2 If I have the gift of prophecy, and know all mysteries and all knowledge; and if I have all faith, so as to remove mountains, but do not have love, I am nothing.

1 Corinthians 13:13 But now faith, hope, love, abide these three; but the greatest of these is love.

1 Corinthians 15:14 And if Christ has not been raised, then our preaching is vain, your faith also is vain.

1 Corinthians 15:17 And if Christ has not been raised, your faith is worthless; you are still in your sins.

1 Corinthians 16:13 Be on the alert, stand firm in the faith, act like men, be strong.

2 Corinthians 1:24 Not that we lord it over your faith, but are workers with you for your joy; for in your faith you are standing firm.

2 Corinthians 4:13 But having the same spirit of faith, according to what is written, "I BELIEVED, THEREFORE I SPOKE," we also believe, therefore we also speak.

2 Corinthians 5:7 For we walk by faith, not by sight.

2 Corinthians 8:7 But just as you abound in everything, in faith and utterance and knowledge and in all earnestness and in the love we inspired in you, see that you abound in this gracious work also.

2 Corinthians 10:15 Not boasting beyond our measure, that is, in other men's labors, but with the hope that as your faith grows, we shall be, within our sphere, enlarged even more by you.

2 Corinthians 13:5 Test yourselves to see if you are in the faith; examine yourselves! Or do you not recognize this about yourselves, that Jesus Christ is in you—unless indeed you fail the test?

Galatians 1:23 But only, they kept hearing, "He who once persecuted us is now preaching the faith which he once tried to destroy."

Galatians 2:16 Nevertheless knowing that a man is not justified by the works of the Law but through faith in Christ Jesus, even we have believed in Christ Jesus, so that we may be justified by faith in Christ and not by the works of the Law; since by the works of the Law no flesh will be justified.

Galatians 2:20 I have been crucified with Christ; and it is no longer I who live, but Christ lives in me; and the life which I now live in the flesh I live by faith in the Son of God, who loved me and gave Himself up for me.

Galatians 3:2 This is the only thing I want to find out from you: did you receive the Spirit by the works of the Law, or by hearing with faith?

Galatians 3:5 Does He who provides you with the Spirit and works miracles among you, do it by the works of the Law, or by hearing with faith?

Galatians 3:7 Therefore, be sure that it is those who are of faith who are sons of Abraham.

Galatians 3:8 The Scripture, foreseeing that God would justify the Gentiles by faith, preached the gospel beforehand to Abraham, saying, "ALL THE NATIONS WILL BE BLESSED IN YOU."

Galatians 3:9 So then those who are of faith are blessed with Abraham, the believer.

Galatians 3:11 Now that no one is justified by the Law before God is evident; for, "THE RIGHTEOUS MAN SHALL LIVE BY FAITH."

Galatians 3:12 However, the Law is not of faith; on the contrary, "HE WHO PRACTICES THEM SHALL LIVE BY THEM."

Galatians 3:14 In order that in Christ Jesus the blessing of Abraham might come to the Gentiles, so that we would receive the promise of the Spirit through faith.

Galatians 3:22 But the Scripture has shut up everyone under sin, so that the promise by faith in Jesus Christ might be given to those who believe.

Galatians 3:23 But before faith came, we were kept in custody under the law, being shut up to the faith which was later to be revealed.

Galatians 3:24 Therefore the Law has become our tutor to lead us to Christ, so that we may be justified by faith.

Galatians 3:25 But now that faith has come, we are no longer under a tutor.

Galatians 3:26 For you are all sons of God through faith in Christ Jesus.

Galatians 5:5 For we through the Spirit, by faith, are waiting for the hope of righteousness.

Galatians 5:6 For in Christ Jesus neither circumcision nor uncircumcision means anything, but faith working through love.

Galatians 5:22 But the fruit of the Spirit is love, joy, peace, patience, kindness, goodness, faithfulness.

Galatians 6:10 So then, while we have opportunity, let us do good to all people, and especially to those who are of the household of the faith.

Ephesians 1:1 Paul, an apostle of Christ Jesus by the will of God, to the saints who are at Ephesus and who are faithful in Christ Jesus.

Ephesians 1:15 For this reason I too, having heard of the faith in the Lord Jesus which exists among you and your love for all the saints.

Ephesians 2:8 For by grace you have been saved through faith; and that not of yourselves, it is the gift of God.

Ephesians 3:12 In whom we have boldness and confident access through faith in Him.

Ephesians 3:17 So that Christ may dwell in your hearts through faith; and that you, being rooted and grounded in love.

Ephesians 4:5 One Lord, one faith, one baptism.

Ephesians 4:13 Until we all attain to the unity of the faith, and of the knowledge of the Son of God, to a mature man, to the measure of the stature which belongs to the fullness of Christ.

Ephesians 6:16 In addition to all, taking up the shield of faith with which you will be able to extinguish all the flaming arrows of the evil one.

Ephesians 6:23 Peace be to the brethren, and love with faith, from God the Father and the Lord Jesus Christ.

Philippians 1:25 Convinced of this, I know that I will remain and continue with you all for your progress and joy in the faith.

Philippians 1:27 Only conduct yourselves in a manner worthy of the gospel of Christ; so that whether I come and see you or remain absent, I may hear of you that you are standing firm in one spirit, with one mind striving together for the faith of the gospel.

Philippians 2:17 But even if I am being poured out as a drink offering upon the sacrifice and service of your faith, I rejoice and share my joy with you all.

Philippians 3:9 And may be found in Him, not having a righteousness of my own derived from the Law, but that which is through faith in Christ, the righteousness which comes from God on the basis of faith.

Colossians 1:2 To the saints and faithful brethren in Christ who are at Colossae: Grace to you and peace from God our Father.

Colossians 1:4 Since we heard of your faith in Christ Jesus and the love which you have for all the saints.

Colossians 1:7 Just as you learned it from Epaphras, our beloved fellow bond-servant, who is a faithful servant of Christ on our behalf.

Colossians 1:23 If indeed you continue in the faith firmly established and steadfast, and not moved away from the hope of the gospel that you have heard, which was proclaimed in all creation under heaven, and of which I, Paul, was made a minister.

Colossians 2:5 For even though I am absent in body, nevertheless I am with you in spirit, rejoicing to see your good discipline and the stability of your faith in Christ.

Colossians 2:7 Having been firmly rooted and now being built up in Him and established in your faith, just as you were instructed, and overflowing with gratitude.

Colossians 2:12 Having been buried with Him in baptism, in which you were also raised up with Him through faith in the working of God, who raised Him from the dead.

Colossians 4:7 As to all my affairs, Tychicus, our beloved brother and faithful servant and fellow bond-servant in the Lord, will bring you information.

Colossians 4:9 And with him Onesimus, our faithful and beloved brother, who is one of your number. They will inform you about the whole situation here.

1 Thessalonians 1:3 Constantly bearing in mind your work of faith and labor of love and steadfastness of hope in our Lord Jesus Christ in the presence of our God and Father.

1 Thessalonians 1:8 For the word of the Lord has sounded forth from you, not only in Macedonia and Achaia, but also in every place your faith toward God has gone forth, so that we have no need to say anything.

1 Thessalonians 3:2 And we sent Timothy, our brother and God's fellow worker in the gospel of Christ, to strengthen and encourage you as to your faith.

1 Thessalonians 3:5 For this reason, when I could endure it no longer, I also sent to find out about your faith, for fear that the tempter might have tempted you, and our labor would be in vain.

1 Thessalonians 3:6 But now that Timothy has come to us from you, and has brought us good news of your faith and love, and that you always think kindly of us, longing to see us just as we also long to see you.

1 Thessalonians 3:7 For this reason, brethren, in all our distress and affliction we were comforted about you through your faith.

1 Thessalonians 3:10 As we night and day keep praying most earnestly that we may see your face, and may complete what is lacking in your faith?

1 Thessalonians 5:8 But since we are of the day, let us be sober, having put on the breastplate of faith and love, and as a helmet, the hope of salvation.

2 Thessalonians 1:3 We ought always to give thanks to God for you, brethren, as is only fitting, because your faith is greatly enlarged, and the love of each one of you toward one another grows ever greater.

2 Thessalonians 1:4 Therefore, we ourselves speak proudly of you among the churches of God for your perseverance and faith in the midst of all your persecutions and afflictions which you endure.

2 Thessalonians 1:11 To this end also we pray for you always, that our God will count you worthy of your calling, and fulfill every desire for goodness and the work of faith with power.

2 Thessalonians 2:13 But we should always give thanks to God for you, brethren beloved by the Lord, because God has chosen you from the beginning for salvation through sanctification by the Spirit and faith in the truth.

2 Thessalonians 3:2 And that we will be rescued from perverse and evil men; for not all have faith.

1 Timothy 1:2 To Timothy, my true child in the faith: Grace, mercy and peace from God the Father and Christ Jesus our Lord.

1 Timothy 1:4 Nor to pay attention to myths and endless genealogies, which give rise to mere speculation rather than furthering the administration of God which is by faith.

1 Timothy 1:5 But the goal of our instruction is love from a pure heart and a good conscience and a sincere faith.

1 Timothy 1:12   I thank Christ Jesus our Lord, who has strengthened me, because He considered me faithful, putting me into service.

1 Timothy 1:14 And the grace of our Lord was more than abundant, with the faith and love which are found in Christ Jesus.

1 Timothy 1:19 Keeping faith and a good conscience, which some have rejected and suffered shipwreck in regard to their faith.

1 Timothy 2:7 For this I was appointed a preacher and an apostle (I am telling the truth, I am not lying) as a teacher of the Gentiles in faith and truth.

1 Timothy 2:15 But women will be preserved through the bearing of children if they continue in faith and love and sanctity with self-restraint.

1 Timothy 3:9 But holding to the mystery of the faith with a clear conscience.

1 Timothy 3:11 Women must likewise be dignified, not malicious gossips, but temperate, faithful in all things.

1 Timothy 3:13 For those who have served well as deacons obtain for themselves a high standing and great confidence in the faith that is in Christ Jesus.

1 Timothy 4:1 But the Spirit explicitly says that in later times some will fall away from the faith, paying attention to deceitful spirits and doctrines of demons.

1 Timothy 4:6 In pointing out these things to the brethren, you will be a good servant of Christ Jesus, constantly nourished on the words of the faith and of the sound doctrine which you have been following.

1 Timothy 4:12 Let no one look down on your youthfulness, but rather in speech, conduct, love, faith and purity, show yourself an example of those who believe.

1 Timothy 5:8 But if anyone does not provide for his own, and especially for those of his household, he has denied the faith and is worse than an unbeliever.

1 Timothy 6:10 For the love of money is a root of all sorts of evil, and some by longing for it have wandered away from the faith and pierced themselves with many griefs.

1 Timothy 6:11 But flee from these things, you man of God, and pursue righteousness, godliness, faith, love, perseversance and gentleness.

1 Timothy 6:12 Fight the good fight of faith; take hold of the eternal life to which you were called, and you made the good confession in the presence of many witnesses.

1 Timothy 6:21 Which some have professed and thus gone astray from the faith. Grace be with you.

2 Timothy 1:5 For I am mindful of the sincere faith within you, which first dwelt in your grandmother Lois and your mother Eunice, and I am sure that it is in you as well.

2 Timothy 1:13 Retain the standard of sound words which you have heard from me, in the faith and love which are in Christ Jesus.

2 Timothy 2:2 The things which you have heard from me in the presence of many witnesses, entrust these to faithful men who will be able to teach others also.

2 Timothy 2:13 If we are faithless, He remains faithful, for He cannot deny Himself.

2 Timothy 2:18 Men who have gone astray from the truth saying that the resurrection has already taken place, and they upset the faith of some.

2 Timothy 2:22 Now flee from youthful lusts and pursue righteousness, faith, love and peace, with those who call on the Lord from a pure heart.

2 Timothy 3:8 Just as Jannes and Jambres opposed Moses, so these men also oppose the truth, men of depraved mind, rejected in regard to the faith.

2 Timothy 3:10 Now you followed my teaching, conduct, purpose, faith, patience, love, perseverance.

2 Timothy 3:15 And that from childhood you have known the sacred writings which are able to give you the wisdom that leads to salvation through faith which is in Christ Jesus.

2 Timothy 4:7 I have fought the good fight, I have finished the course, I have kept the faith.

Titus 1:1 Paul, a bond-servant of God and an apostle of Jesus Christ, for the faith of those chosen of God and the knowledge of the truth which is according to godliness.

Titus 1:4 To Titus, my true child in a common faith: Grace and peace from God the Father and Christ Jesus our Savior.

Titus 1:9 Holding fast the faithful word which is in accordance with the teaching, so that he will be able both to exhort in sound doctrine and to refute those who contradict.

Titus 1:13 This testimony is true. For this reason reprove them severely so that they may be sound in the faith.

Titus 2:2 Older men are to be temperate, dignified, sensible, sound in faith, in love, in perseverance.

Titus 2:10 Not pilfering, but showing all good faith so that they will adorn the doctrine of God our Savior in every respect.

Titus 3:15 All who are with me greet you. Greet those who love us in the faith. Grace be with you all.

Philemon 1:5 Because I hear of your love and of the faith which you have toward the Lord Jesus, and toward all the saints.

Philemon 1:6 And I pray that the fellowship of your faith may become effective through the knowledge of every good thing which is in you for Christ's sake.

Hebrews 4:2 For indeed we have had good news preached to us, just as they also; but the word they heard did not profit them, because it was not united by faith in those who heard.

Hebrews 6:1 Therefore leaving the elementary teaching about the Christ, let us press on to maturity, not laying again a foundation of repentance from dead works and of faith toward God.

Hebrews 6:12 That you will not be sluggish, but imitators of those who through faith and patience inherit the promises.

Hebrews 10:22 Let us draw near with a sincere heart in full assurance of faith, having our hearts sprinkled clean from an evil conscience and our bodies washed with pure water.

Hebrews 10:23 Let us hold fast the confession of our hope without wavering, for He who promised is faithful.

Hebrews 10:38 BUT MY RIGHTEOUS ONE SHALL LIVE BY FAITH; AND IF HE SHRINKS BACK, MY SOUL HAS NO PLEASURE IN HIM.

Hebrews 10:39 But we are not of those who shrink back to destruction, but of those who have faith to the preserving of the soul.

Hebrews 11:1 Now faith is the assurance of things hoped for, the conviction of things not seen.

Hebrews 11:3 By faith we understand that the worlds were prepared by the word of God, so that what is seen was not made out of things which are visible.

Hebrews 11:4 By faith Abel offered to God a better sacrifice than Cain, through which he obtained the testimony that he was righteous, God testifying about his gifts, and through faith, though he is dead, he still speaks.

Hebrews 11:5 By faith Enoch was taken up so that he would not see death; AND HE WAS NOT FOUND BECAUSE GOD TOOK HIM UP; for he obtained the witness that before his being taken up he was pleasing to God.

Hebrews 11:6 And without faith it is impossible to please Him, for he who comes to God must believe that He is and that He is a rewarder of those who seek Him.

Hebrews 11:7 By faith Noah, being warned by God about things not yet seen, in reverence prepared an ark for the salvation of his household, by which he condemned the world, and became an heir of the righteousness which is according to faith.

Hebrews 11:8 By faith Abraham, when he was called, obeyed by going out to a place which he was to receive for an inheritance; and he went out, not knowing where he was going.

Hebrews 11:9 By faith he lived as an alien in the land of promise, as in a foreign land, dwelling in tents with Isaac and Jacob, fellow heirs of the same promise.

Hebrews 11:11 By faith even Sarah herself received ability to conceive, even beyond the proper time of life, since she considered Him faithful who had promised.

Hebrews 11:13 All these died in faith, without receiving the promises, but having seen them and having welcomed them from a distance, and having confessed that they were strangers and exiles on the earth.

Hebrews 11:17 By faith Abraham, when he was tested, offered up Isaac, and he who had received the promises was offering up his only begotten son.

Hebrews 11:20 By faith Isaac blessed Jacob and Esau, even regarding things to come.

Hebrews 11:21 By faith Jacob, as he was dying, blessed each of the sons of Joseph, and worshiped, leaning on the top of his staff.

Hebrews 11:22 By faith Joseph, when he was dying, made mention of the exodus of the sons of Israel, and gave orders concerning his bones.

Hebrews 11:23 By faith Moses, when he was born, was hidden for three months by his parents, because they saw he was a beautiful child; and they were not afraid of the king's edict.

Hebrews 11:24 By faith Moses, when he had grown up, refused to be called the son of Pharaoh's daughter.

Hebrews 11:27 By faith he left Egypt, not fearing the wrath of the king; for he endured, as seeing Him who is unseen.

Hebrews 11:28 By faith he kept the Passover and the sprinkling of the blood, so that he who destroyed the firstborn would not touch them.

Hebrews 11:29 By faith they passed through the Red Sea as though they were passing through dry land; and the Egyptians, when they attempted it, were drowned.

Hebrews 11:30 By faith the walls of Jericho fell down after they had been encircled for seven days.

Hebrews 11:31 By faith Rahab the harlot did not perish along with those who were disobedient, after she had welcomed the spies in peace.

Hebrews 11:33 Who by faith conquered kingdoms, performed acts of righteousness, obtained promises, shut the mouths of lions.

Hebrews 11:39 And all these, having gained approval through their faith, did not receive what was promised.

Hebrews 12:2 Fixing our eyes on Jesus, the author and perfecter of faith, who for the joy set before Him endured the cross, despising the shame, and has sat down at the right hand of the throne of God.

Hebrews 13:7 Remember those who led you, who spoke the word of God to you; and considering the result of their conduct, imitate their faith.

James 1:3 Knowing that the testing of your faith produces endurance.

James 1:6 But he must ask in faith without any doubting, for the one who doubts is like the surf of the sea driven and tossed by the wind.

James 2:1 My brethren, do not hold your faith in our glorious Lord Jesus Christ with an attitude of personal favoritism.

James 2:5 Listen, my beloved brethren: did not God choose the poor of this world to be rich in faith and heirs of the kingdom which He promised to those who love Him?

James 2:14 What use is it, my brethren, if someone says he has faith but he has no works? Can that faith save him?

James 2:17 Even so faith, if it has no works, is dead, being by itself.

James 2:18 But someone may well say, "You have faith and I have works; show me your faith without the works, and I will show you my faith by my works."

James 2:20 But are you willing to recognize, you foolish fellow, that faith without works is useless?

James 2:22 You see that faith was working with his works, and as a result of the works, faith was perfected.

James 2:24 You see that a man is justified by works and not by faith alone.

James 2:26 For just as the body without the spirit is dead, so also faith without works is dead.

James 5:15 And the prayer offered in faith will restore the one who is sick, and the Lord will raise him up, and if he has committed sins, they will be forgiven him.

1 Peter 1:5 Who are protected by the power of God through faith for a salvation ready to be revealed in the last time.

1 Peter 1:7 So that the proof of your faith, being more precious than gold which is perishable, even though tested by fire, may be found to result in praise and glory and honor at the revelation of Jesus Christ.

1 Peter 1:9 Obtaining as the outcome of your faith the salvation of your souls.

1 Peter 1:21 Who through Him are believers in God, who raised Him from the dead and gave Him glory, so that your faith and hope are in God.

1 Peter 4:19 Therefore, those also who suffer according to the will of God shall entrust their souls to a faithful Creator in doing what is right.

1 Peter 5:9 But resist him, firm in your faith, knowing that the same experiences of suffering are being accomplished by your brethren who are in the world.

1 Peter 5:12 Through Silvanus, our faithful brother (for so I regard him), I have written to you briefly, exhorting and testifying that this is the true grace of God. Stand firm in it!

2 Peter 1:1 Simon Peter, a bond-servant and apostle of Jesus Christ, to those who have received a faith of the same kind as ours, by the righteousness of our God and Savior, Jesus Christ.

2 Peter 1:5 Now for this very reason also, applying all diligence, in your faith supply moral excellence, and in your moral excellence, knowledge.

1 John 1:9 If we confess our sins, He is faithful and righteous to forgive us our sins and to cleanse us from all unrighteousness.

1 John 5:4 For whatever is born of God overcomes the world; and this is the victory that has overcome the world—our faith.

3 John 1:5 Beloved, you are acting faithfully in whatever you accomplish for the brethren, and especially when they are strangers.

Jude 1:3 Beloved, while I was making every effort to write you about our common salvation, I felt the necessity to write to you appealing that you contend earnestly for the faith which was once for all handed down to the saints.

Jude 1:20 But you, beloved, building yourselves up on your most holy faith, praying in the Holy Spirit.

Revelation 1:5 And from Jesus Christ, the faithful witness, the firstborn of the dead, and the ruler of the kings of the earth. To Him who loves us and released us from our sins by His blood.

Revelation 2:10 Do not fear what you are about to suffer. Behold, the devil is about to cast some of you into prison, so that you will be tested, and you will have tribulation for ten days. Be faithful until death, and I will give you the crown of life.

Revelation 2:13 I know where you dwell, where Satan's throne is; and you hold fast My name, and did not deny My faith even in the days of Antipas, My witness, My faithful one, who was killed among you, where Satan dwells.

Revelation 2:19 I know your deeds, and your love and faith and service and perseverance, and that your deeds of late are greater than at first.

Revelation 3:14 To the angel of the church in Laodicea write: The Amen, the faithful and true Witness, the Beginning of the creation of God, says this.

Revelation 13:10 If anyone is destined for captivity, to captivity he goes; if anyone kills with the sword, with the sword he must be killed. Here is the perseverance and the faith of the saints.

Revelation 14:12 Here is the perseverance of the saints who keep the commandments of God and their faith in Jesus.

Revelation 17:14 "These will wage war against the Lamb, and the Lamb will overcome them, because He is Lord of lords and King of kings, and those who are with Him are the called and chosen and faithful."

Revelation 19:11 And I saw heaven opened, and behold, a white horse, and He who sat on it is called Faithful and True, and in righteousness He judges and wages war.

Revelation 21:5 And He who sits on the throne said, "Behold, I am making all things new." And He said, "Write, for these words are faithful and true."

Revelation 22:6 And he said to me, "These words are faithful and true"; and the Lord, the God of the spirits of the prophets, sent His angel to show to His bond-servants the things which must soon take place.